REFUGEE HIGH

REFUGEE HIGH

COMING OF AGE IN AMERICA

ELLY FISHMAN

THE
NEW
PRESS

NEW YORK
LONDON

Published in the United States by The New Press, New York, 2021
Distributed by Two Rivers Distribution

ISBN 978-1-62097-508-4 (hc)
ISBN 978-1-62097-509-1 (ebook)
CIP data is available

The New Press publishes books that promote and enrich public discussion and understanding of the issues vital to our democracy and to a more equitable world. These books are made possible by the enthusiasm of our readers; the support of a committed group of donors, large and small; the collaboration of our many partners in the independent media and the not-for-profit sector; booksellers, who often hand-sell New Press books; librarians; and above all by our authors.

www.thenewpress.com

INTERNATIONAL WOMEN'S MEDIA FOUNDATION This reporting was supported by the International Women's Media Foundation's Howard G. Buffett Fund For Women Journalists

Book design and composition by Bookbright Media
This book was set in Minion and Futura

Printed in the United States of America

10 9 8 7 6 5 4 3 2 1

For my family

CONTENTS

FEATURING

Mariah, a sophomore from Basra, Iraq
Fatmeh, her mother
Farha, her older sister
Khalil, her father

Alejandro, a senior and asylum seeker from Guatemala City,
    Guatemala
Sergio, his father
Luana, his mother
Jose, his best friend

Belenge, a Congolese sophomore born in Nyarugusu, a
    refugee camp in Kigoma, Tanzania
Esengo, his friend and a Congolese refugee
Tobias, his father
Asani, his brother
Felix, his friend, neighbor, and a Congolese refugee
Mama Sakina, Felix's mother

Shahina, a sophomore from Yangon, Myanmar
Aishah, her best friend and a Burmese refugee

Zakiah, her mother

Nassim, a freshman from Daraa, Syria
Abdul Karim, a senior from Homs, Syria
Samir, a senior from Homs, Syria

Chad Adams, the principal of Roger C. Sullivan High School
Sarah Quintenz, the director of the Sullivan High School
English language learner program
Matt Fasana, the assistant principal at Sullivan High School
Josh Zepeda, the English language learner social worker at
Sullivan High School
Danny Rizk, a math and science teacher's aide at Sullivan
High School

REFUGEE HIGH

1

SEPTEMBER

Mariah

Mariah can't sleep. Tomorrow is her first day at Sullivan High School. Staring up at the underbelly of the top bunk occupied by her younger sister, Mariah considers the outfit she's picked out for her first day: white jeans, a blue and white shirt, and blue Converse sneakers with white trim and white laces. She's also decided to wear her hijab again, this time with style. Mariah picked out a black scarf, which she plans to wrap into a turban. She's anxious about starting at a new school. What will it be like? Will there be drama? Will life at Sullivan prove better than at the huge suburban high school where she barely survived her freshman year?

Sometimes when Mariah lies awake, she tries to revisit her memories from Basra, the coastal city in Iraq where she was born, but left at age ten. The fifteen-year-old doesn't recall much, but she likes to replay what she does. She remembers walking down the street with her eldest sister. Men would often approach her sister, something Mariah, whose arched eyebrows and barbed spirit have made her a favorite among high school boys, only understood once she got older. She remembers going to school and fearing traveling alone to the outdoor shower.

Soon, Mariah shifts back to her surroundings. The bedroom remains still. It's quieter now that Mariah's seventeen-year-old sister Farha moved to Atlanta to marry. But Mariah still shares the room with two of her sisters and their bedroom is rarely this peaceful—Mariah's arms are dotted with scars, all of them battle wounds from hair-pulling, shin-kicking fights. Before Farha left, Mariah was close with her older sister. That was before everything went sour last year. The thought saddens Mariah, but she isn't one to dwell. Farha is gone and Mariah gets a fresh start.

Chad Adams

Chad Adams sits at the edge of his bed. The heat, which he feels rising from the floor, suggests that summer lingers. But the sunless sky reveals the truth: fall waits just around the corner. Chad has always loved the first day of school. As principal of Roger C. Sullivan High School, Chad gets to hit reset every September. It's like New Year's Eve, but better. And by his own logic, today marks Chad's fifteenth shot at reinvention.

Planting his feet on the ground, Chad begins to visualize the day ahead of him. He imagines the school facade, marked by red bricks and white stone carved with modern gothic finishes. The building is large with two wings, each of which stretches out from the central lobby and covers nearly half a city block. The sign out front welcomes the students back and shines with the hope of a promising new year. Inside, the forty-one-year-old imagines himself in the auditorium welcoming new students and high-fiving those returning. Chad sees himself talking to parents, assuring them their kids are in good hands. He pokes his head into classrooms to check in on teachers. He jokes around with the security staff, who are stationed on every floor.

Visualizing the day helps Chad feel prepared. Without opening his blue eyes, he begins his mantra—the same one he practices each morning: *I am calm. I am calm. I am calm.* As he repeats the line in his head, he can feel his body—shoulders, chest, stomach—relax. He lets the weight of his body sink into the mattress. He feels heavier with each repetition. Chad inhales through his nose and breathes out of his mouth. He repeats the mantra for a full minute. When he finishes, Chad turns his attention to his toes. He starts his third exercise of the morning. *I am noticing my feet,* he says to himself. He holds the thought for a few seconds before letting it dissipate. *I am noticing my ankles. I am noticing my calves. My knees.* Chad crawls his way to the tip of his head. When he acknowledges each part of his body, he opens his eyes. Chad begins every day like this—he has to.

Just after 6:30 a.m., Chad zigzags his way into the Rogers Park neighborhood. The rainy summer has turned the already verdant blocks surrounding Sullivan High School an even richer array of greens. In the remaining few blocks of his commute, Chad passes rows of blocky, heavily corniced two-flat apartment buildings and nineteenth-century Victorian homes. The neighborhood is marked by a smattering of murals that celebrate native lake fish and the popular local cartoon character Fly Boy. He passes signs, wet with dew, that read Hate Has No Home Here, and rainbow flags pinned to first-floor window frames. Few sounds travel across the neighborhood at this early hour. Only the elevated Red Line train drums a clicking bass line as it rolls to and from the Loyola and Morse Avenue stops. Soon, street traffic will start to pick up. The Ethiopian cafe, Royal Coffee, will open its doors at 7 a.m. and later the Cuban grocery store La Unica will welcome its first customers of the day. But for now, Chad lets the early-morning serenity sink in.

Wearing a slim black suit with his shaggy blond hair hanging at his shoulders, Chad punches his four-digit employee code into one of the school's heavy steel doors. The halls are quiet; only the custodians and the front desk clerk precede him here. On his way to school, Chad listened as President Trump threatened to end the Deferred Action for Childhood Arrivals (DACA), a program created by the Obama administration that gives immigrant youth brought to the United States unlawfully the temporary right to legally live, study, and work in America. Spanish is the second-most-spoken language at Sullivan, and Chad knows the school serves several Dreamers.

In the nine months since Donald Trump took office, he's been a source of fear at Sullivan. As soon as his term began, the Forty-Fifth, as Chad calls him, started a campaign to reduce the number of immigrants, refugees, and asylum seekers entering the United States. In January, he announced a travel ban barring citizens from seven Muslim-majority countries from entering the country. He pushed to allot $18 billion toward building a wall along the U.S.–Mexico border and prioritized the prosecution of criminal immigrant violations such as illegal entry. Chad knows that such rhetoric could have a ripple effect and shake students living in already tenuous circumstances. And there are a lot of such kids at Sullivan. More than half the students, or over three hundred kids, came to the United States as immigrants or refugees.

At 7:30 a.m., students start to pour into the hallways. Groups of girls in hijabs squeal as they greet one another. Congolese mothers, clad in bright Liputa dresses, admonish their children to stay nearby. Boys from the football team arrive in packs, their shouts to one another cutting across the wall of sounds. In many ways, Sullivan, which is small by Chicago public school standards, operates like several mini schools within the same building. Immigrant and refugee students tend to stick together and to classrooms that sit in the North Wing of the school. Their American-born classmates, by contrast, tribe up based on sports teams, school clubs, grade levels, and academic tracks such as the medical and business programs, and ROTC. Chad's job includes finding ways to unify the various populations. He wants everyone to feel proud to wear Sullivan's uniform and that Sullivan is their school.

Standing just inside the front doors, Chad can feel the potent mix of first-day jitters and excitement. He tries to greet every student who enters. Chad exudes casual confidence. He is Sullivan's best salesman.

Thirty minutes later, Chad takes the stage in the school auditorium. The room is near silent except for the low murmurs of new freshmen who fill the first few rows. Chad, looking out at a string of international flags that hang off the balcony, pulls the microphone to his mouth. He quickly clears his throat. He's always clearing his throat, a habit that verges on compulsive.

Welcome, freshmen! It's great to meet you. Chad looks out onto the new students. Who will they become, he wonders. *We're here to help you. Use the resources of your school. Use your teachers. Use everyone you can to help you this year whenever you're struggling. And whenever you need something, make sure you come to me. My name is Mr. Adams and I'm the principal. I'm in 215. My office is right in the middle of the school. . . . At Sullivan we really try not to solve our problems with our fists.* Chad scrunches his hand into a fist and holds it up. *Because this leads to this.* Chad contorts his hand into a gun shape. *Which leads to this.* He points his hand toward the ground. *At Sullivan we try and use our heads and our hearts.* He releases the gun shape and motions to his temples and chest. *But I also want you to know that I have the biggest security guard in the district and no one is entering this school without a warrant, no matter what the Forty-Fifth is saying outside these walls. . . . Have a great day today.*

Mariah

When Mariah's alarm rings, she guesses she got less than four hours of sleep. Fatmeh, Mariah's mother, accompanies the new sophomore to her first day. As soon as the two are through the front doors, Mariah notes the two metal detectors, which form a prison-like barrier to the school. Like every student in front of her, Mariah must put her backpack on a conveyor belt where it is screened under an X-ray machine. Fatmeh tells her daughter the machinery reminds her of the airport.

Once inside, Mariah surveys the hall. She hears Arabic and soon spots a cluster of girls wearing hijabs. Sullivan, she thinks to herself, is nothing like her previous school. Someone directs Mariah and Fatmeh to the school library, a space that has become a landing place, and waiting area, for the school's refugee families. Inside, smatterings of Arabic-speaking parents gather around tables to the south. Mothers clad in hijabs and long dresses seem to wilt in the near ninety-degree heat. Together, their conversations swing from laughter and gossip to fierce disciplinary outcries. On the western edge of the room, where desktop computers form a line just below the windows, a group of Burmese families hunch in metal chairs that suit their small frames. A few Latino boys sit at the center of the room. One brags that his fake ID got him a job at Dunkin Donuts, and the other sheepishly admits that he was fired from the sandwich shop Jimmy Johns. In the northeastern section of the room, African families, most of them Congolese, crowd a corner.

Only a few minutes pass before Mariah hears her name.

"What? Mariah? I'm so confused," says Josh Zepeda, the newly hired social worker for the English language learner program. Josh spent a year working as a social worker at the same high school north of Chicago where Mariah finished her freshman year.

"What are you doing here?"

"What are *you* doing here, Mr. Zepeda?" Mariah snaps back. "You changed schools?"

"Yeah, I did."

"Why?"

"Oh, it just wasn't the place for me."

"Me either."

Mariah surveys the room. She suddenly feels shy. Following Fatmeh, Mariah takes a seat and waits.

Alejandro

Alejandro never leaves for school without perfecting his hair. The eighteen-year-old Guatemalan always keeps his curls combed up into a square, well-defined pompadour that sweeps upward from his forehead and drops into a frizzy ponytail in back. Alejandro also sports a pencil mustache and bushy strap of hair along the length of his lower lip. He likes to look good and the facial hair projects maturity. He rotates between fitted jeans—including a pair of bright white ones with ripped knees—and heather gray sweatpants, which he might pair with a soccer jersey or a matching tightly fitted shirt. Alejandro's future in the United States may be tenuous, but that's not a reason to stifle his sense of style or the quietly confident way he moves in unsure space.

Most days, Alejandro walks to school. He likes to walk. In Guatemala City, walking through the blocks claimed by rival gangs could feel like an act of resistance. Varying his route helped him stay free, for a while, of gang violence. In Chicago, Alejandro walks the same twenty-five-minute route to school almost every day. On his way he passes a yard full of sculptures made from scrap metal and a neighborhood vendor who hawks smoothies and plastic cups filled with fruit. He passes McDonald's and a taco joint he knows well. The salsa is especially spicy and the television plays soccer matches all day long.

Now a senior at Sullivan High School, Alejandro feels more assured there than ever. He knows where all the classes are, and what teachers he likes and which ones he dreads. He knows he'll never eat the cafeteria food even though the lunch is free. Sarah Quintenz, his former and favorite teacher, makes daily runs to 7-Eleven, and if he gives her a few dollars, she brings him a hot dog or slice of pizza. Alejandro knows that this year the school counselors will push him to map out his future after Sullivan. He'll apply to a few community colleges. His bigger plan is to be a master plumber or mechanic.

But Alejandro's life also comes with some terrifying "ifs" that may well wreck his planned adulthood. Before Alejandro fled Guatemala in 2013, he spent months feeling like he was being hunted. He'd often spot cars tailing him on his way home from school. That's why he never walked the same paths twice. He stopped going to restaurants, and rarely left the house. Gang members from MS-13, or the Mara Salvatrucha gang, he feared, were watching him to kill him. In the logic of Guatemala's gangland, Alejandro's life would be a price his family paid for not giving in to thugs. At just thirteen years old, Alejandro felt alternatively like a prisoner or like prey. If he returns to Guatemala now, Alejandro feels certain he'd face the same threat, and likely, death. Maybe the judge he meets on November 11 will believe Alejandro's fears are real and give him asylee status in the United States. It's a last chance for him. This will be his second, and final, plea for asylum.

Belenge

Pausing just inside the metal detectors, Belenge, who has arrived with his younger brother, Asani, stands frozen at the edge of the Sullivan hallways. The fast-moving stream of students bends around the boys. Belenge and Asani are no strangers to chaos. They were raised in a world colored by makeshift shelters and scarcity of wood, food, and water. Like many young Congolese refugees, the two were born as stateless citizens in the only hospital inside Nyarugusu, the sprawling refugee camp in Kigoma, Tanzania. They grew up among more than 150,000 people without a place to call home. But here, in the hallways of Sullivan, where the crowds of students include groups of tall, broad-shouldered Syrian teenagers, pairs of girls in headscarves and trench coats, and kids with Apple headphones and pristine Jordans, Belenge does not yet understand his place in the school's social order.

Belenge has been anticipating his first day of school all summer. He picked out red track pants and a black striped jacket for his first-day outfit. He arrived in Chicago twelve months ago and spent last year at the nearby Senn High School. There, he sat in the back of regular classes. Belenge, who still struggles to communicate and express himself in English, couldn't follow the lessons. He also found the rigid structure—long hours, strict attendance policies, nightly homework—frustrating.

Everything overwhelmed Belenge when he first arrived in the United States. Belenge and his family had never lived in an apartment. He never had electricity nor seen a three-story building. He'd never used a refrigerator or walked into a room full of books. He'd never seen snow or worn a winter coat. Cell phones and social media were novel, too. But enrolling at a new school introduced Belenge to a new, social anxiety: fitting in. The sixteen-year-old discovered that strangers often assumed he was Black American. But to Belenge, Black students were just as foreign to him as any of his other American classmates.

Not long after Belenge and Asani arrive at Sullivan, a youth manager joins them. She's from RefugeeOne, the resettlement agency that helped Belenge and his family establish their lives in Chicago. Taking a few steps into the hallway, the counselor shepherds the brothers toward the library. Inside, Belenge spots a coterie of Bembe Congolese families in the corner. His entire body relaxes and he smiles, revealing a set of brilliant white teeth. Among the group, Belenge sees his friends Esengo and Felix. Both boys are also from Nyarugusu. Esengo sits with his sister whose feet are squeezed into high heels and whose eyes and cheekbones are accentuated by thick makeup. She looks like a soap opera star. Felix, who started at Sullivan last year, nods to Belenge. Felix's English is good thanks to hours spent watching American movies, listening to pop music, and reading American books. Belenge figures Felix probably knows every lyric to every Justin Bieber song by now.

Felix and Belenge make a plan to walk home together. The two are neighbors now that Belenge's father moved his family next door to Felix's family's apartment. Belenge's father, Tobias, works long hours and when he isn't working, he drinks. Felix's mother, Sakina, who everyone calls Mama Sakina, looks after Belenge and his siblings. She makes them *fufu* in the afternoon and spends the evening braiding Belenge's sister's hair. In an environment where everything remains new, Mama Sakina offers Belenge some sense of stability.

After greeting his friends, Belenge takes a seat in the library. A student explains, in Swahili, that he needs to wait for his schedule. Belenge settles in. He doesn't mind waiting. He's used to it. In Nyarugusu, the average family remains in the camp for seventeen years before they are resettled somewhere new. Waiting is part of life.

Shahina

Every morning on her way to Sullivan High School, Shahina passes reminders of the life she narrowly escaped. That's why she counts down the days until she turns eighteen. She still has 408 days to go, but that's close enough to keep the Burmese sophomore in good spirits.

Though the way to school conjures bitter memories, Shahina, a refugee from Myanmar, is always relieved to be out of the house. Tensions are high at home—Shahina and her mother rarely speak, and when they do, Zakiah curses her daughter's obstinacy—and school offers distraction. Inside Sullivan, Shahina walks past quotes painted next to each classroom. Maya Lin's "The American Dream is being able to follow your calling" and one from Dr. Seuss: "Think left and think right and think low and think high. Oh, the thinks you can think up if only you try!" The school is a sea of navy blue lockers with the bright yellow *S*, Sullivan's insignia, painted above them. Below, the drab black-and-brown-checkered floors seem to dampen the optimism advertised on the walls.

The deteriorating first-floor girls' bathroom, marked by large concrete slabs and rusting water pipes, stands among Shahina's most cherished spaces inside Sullivan. It's there, in the fetid room, that the sixteen-year-old will station herself near the mirror and take dozens of hijab-less selfies. She'll spend hours each day posting photos enhanced by kitten-ear filters to Snapchat, uploading close-up doe-eyed portraits to Instagram, and keeping up with ongoing flirtations with a slew of Burmese boys on Facebook Messenger. Recently she's been talking to a Rohingya boy in Boston who claims he carries a gun and runs with a crew called the Asian Boyz Gang. His profile picture boasts the group's logo: their name with a lightning bolt for a *z*.

Though she's never been particularly interested in school, Shahina looks forward to starting her sophomore year at Sullivan. At school, she can watch YouTube tutorials on sunset makeup looks and catch up on social media gossip. She can make plans to watch scary movies and hitch a ride to the mall. She can drink Diet Coke and eat soggy pizza. Ever since Shahina, who cloaks her thin frame with loose clothing, began fighting with her mother, the girl refuses to eat at home. Most days, the meals provided at school are the only ones she eats.

At Sullivan, Shahina can be a kid. Six months ago, the teenager thought she'd never get that chance again.

Chad Adams

Chad leaves the auditorium at 8:10 a.m. He heads directly toward the school lobby. There, he passes a wall of notable Sullivan graduates—Borscht Belt comedian Shecky Greene, cinematographer Haskell Wexler, Congresswoman Jan Schakowsky, Pulitzer Prize–winner Ira Berkow, and an assortment of local luminaries. The images signal Sullivan's roots in serving immigrant and first-generation children since it opened in 1929. For nearly a century, Sullivan has been an engine of education and integration for immigrants.

The first editions of the yearbook, called *The Navillus*, or Sullivan spelled backward, are dotted with images of students like Rhoda Rothbaum, a brown-eyed young woman with glossy lips and a center part, and Robert Gluckman, a serious-looking young man who participated in both the business and economic clubs. Back then, Sullivan students would gather at Ashkenaz's Deli on Morse Avenue, a joint known across town for its corned beef on rye. On the weekends, sophomore and junior boys would gather at Fratini's, a bowling alley and pool hall for men only.

Later, in the 1970s, the school population shifted as Vietnamese and Cambodian refugees began to resettle in the neighborhood. By the late 1980s Sullivan served a majority Black American population, which remained true for the next two decades. When Chad first walked through the doors of Sullivan in 2013, the school had been on probation for thirteen years running. It also had the highest number of in-school violent incidents on the north side of the city. He was the fourth principal in five years. Sullivan was a place that had suffered from troubled leadership and decades of divestment. That meant if it didn't improve academically, and attract more students, the school could be shuttered for good.

In his first year at Sullivan, Chad took note of another characteristic that made the school unique. He noticed that the student population included kids from all over the world. Though Chad had spent his career working in public schools, he'd never encountered such a diverse student body. One reason Sullivan boasted a global population, Chad would learn, was that Chicago's five major refugee resettlement agencies, groups that work with the United Nations High Commissioner for Refugees to sponsor and support new American families once they reach the United States, were located on the North Side of the city. Resettlement agencies help connect new refugees to jobs, medical and financial support, food stamps, and schools. They also set up families in apartments and cover the first three months of rent after families arrive in the United States. In Chicago, that means that most refugee families are placed in apartments not far from East Rogers

Park, an area that keeps them close to the agencies and makes Sullivan their neighborhood school.

Chad saw an opportunity. He wanted Sullivan to serve not only families resettled in the neighborhood, but all the teenage refugees arriving in Chicago, too. He understood that finding a new mission for the school could turn Sullivan's fate around. In his second year as principal, he decided to allocate extra funds to the school's English language learner, or ELL, program, designed for refugee and immigrants who speak little or no English. Five years later, more than 70 percent of the students speak a second language, and over half of the students are either in, or have graduated from, an ELL program. There are close to forty languages spoken at Sullivan. And among students, Arabic is the third-most-spoken language after English and Spanish. One nickname for Sullivan: the Google Translate School. Some students need the app to talk to others.

Passing through the lobby, Chad makes his way to the tower, the highest point in the school, which sits at the building's center. He comes here to absorb the energy of the school. Chad believes in spirits—he burns sage at home when he feels the presence of a nasty one—and Sullivan is full of them, and not just those whose names hang on the walls. Standing at the top of the tower stairs, Chad leans into the bannister. He lets the commotion below rise to meet him. Over the last four years, Sullivan's performance ranking has steadily risen. Today marks the start of Chad's fifth year as principal at the Rogers Park high school, which means he has made it halfway through his ten-year plan to turn the once-troubled neighborhood school around. When Chad pitched the local school council, he promised that by 2023, Sullivan would be a school where he'd send his own son. Shaping Sullivan into a good school—in his first five years Sullivan has risen from Level 3, the lowest Chicago Public Schools ranking, to a 2-plus—has been the hardest work of Chad's career. But Chad intends to turn Sullivan into a *great* neighborhood high school. That transformation will be his legacy. He holds the image in his mind and lets the thought propel him back down the stairs.

Sarah Quintenz

It's not yet 11 a.m., and Sarah Quintenz has already sought stillness in her car three times today.

Sitting in the driver's seat of her midnight blue Toyota with the window rolled halfway down, Sarah holds her cigarette and releases a long exhale of smoke. On a whim this morning, Sarah decided to wear flared white jeans, a decision she's now regretting. They get dirty easily, and she's been rubbing a lot of elbows. As usual, Sarah is frustrated with the cell phone service inside the Sullivan building, but now sees all the messages that sat in purgatory arrive in a rapid-fire succession. She scans each message but waits to respond. Enjoying her smoke, Sarah soaks in the melancholy notes of the Dave Matthews Band song "Crash into Me," which plays from her car stereo.

After five years teaching in the English language learner program, Sarah has stepped into a new role: director of Sullivan's recently created Newcomer Center, the first within Chicago Public Schools. The designation is especially for schools that offer robust, targeted programming for refugee and immigrant students and comes as a response to the steady rise of refugee students at Sullivan over the past two years. At the end of the 2016–17 school year, more than one hundred new refugees enrolled at Sullivan. It also means an additional $300,000 funding for ELL education, which helps cover seven new teachers and staff who all report to Sarah. Sullivan's refugee and immigrant students are geographically, religiously, and culturally diverse. They stand among those caught in what's been called the worst refugee crisis in history with more than fifty million people across the globe fleeing violence or other threats. Her students arrive from more than thirty countries and some have lived their whole prior lives in refugee camps. Nearly all have been subject to the world at its most hateful and violent. Students can sit in the hall and compare notes on the relatives they've seen killed in front of them. Most are traumatized. Many are highly resilient; some are less so. The Sullivan staff's task is not only to teach them English, but to figure out ways to help this current crop of refugee students leave high school as a formidable new generation.

_____

But for now, Sarah just has to make it through the first day. She takes a final drag of her cigarette. She arrived at school already tired. It hasn't been an easy year for the thirty-seven-year-old. In June, she finalized her divorce after a two-year separation. The process has left her with debt and deep wounds. Sarah is still waiting for her life to feel less painful.

Back inside the school, Sarah, who is thin with an angled, cropped haircut and dark brown eyes, keeps pace. She only makes it a few feet before hearing her name shouted across the hall.

"Ms. Q!" a round-faced sophomore in a hijab, a refugee from Myanmar, throws her arms around Sarah's waist.

"Hi, honey. How was your summer?" Sarah responds, though she doesn't expect an entirely honest answer. After years of working with refugees, Sarah has learned that the truth doesn't always emerge right away. Students juggle numerous challenges and often conceal home pressures. Among them, arranged marriages, a practice that hits Sarah especially hard. That's one reason Sarah, who uses pitch-black humor to connect with students, ends every school week by offering the students the idiom: "Have a good weekend. Don't get pregnant. Love you!"

"Good. Boring," the girl responds, her hands now hooked on her backpack straps.

"Come say hi later," says Sarah. "I'm in the library now."

Sarah's new office, which she shares with three other staff, sits at the northern corner of the library. Before she heads to the small, claustrophobic room, Sarah scans the library for her new hires. Josh Zepeda speaks in Spanish with a freshman boy who looks on the verge of tears. He manages to get a laugh out of the boy, which seems nothing short of a small miracle. Danny Rizk, the frenetic twenty-three-year-old math and science tutor, translates for a Muslim family in a blend of the Egyptian Arabic he learned from his great-aunt and Syrian phrases he picked up during his time as one of Sullivan's City Year fellows. The goal today is to register as many students as possible. Sarah has registered scores of new immigrant and refugee students at Sullivan. She speeds through the process faster than anyone else. Every few feet, she stops to give a quick, three-question assessment test: *How are you? What country are you from? How old are you?* In a matter of seconds, Sarah can determine enough information to temporarily place them in one of the school's four introductory ELL tracks. She will later administer the formal placement test, but for now her goal is to get new students into the classroom as quickly as possible. After a few short rounds, she arrives at a boy slumped in the corner of the room.

"Hi, how are you?" she asks. He mumbles a response, his eyes downcast at the floor. The boy's plastic backpack protrudes from his back. Sarah stands her ground, unphased. Sarah prides herself on crafting pointed responses that cut through the fog, and surly teenagers are her specialty.

"Hey, I need you to look at me when I talk to you," she continues.

The boy briefly makes eye contact before darting his gaze to the corner of the room. "There you go," she says encouragingly. "Was that so hard?"

He laughs. A couple more questions answered, and Sarah discovers the boy has lived in the United States for eight years. He doesn't require ELL classes.

"Sometimes they don't speak English, and sometimes they're just dumb teenagers," Sarah grumbles. Within seconds, she's on to the next.

2

OCTOBER 13

Belenge

As on most days early in the school year, Belenge starts Friday, October 13, at the glass bus shelter on the intersection of Birchwood Avenue and Clark Street. He waits for a few of the other Congolese refugee students to meet at the corner before the group makes its daily trek the 1.2 miles south to Sullivan.

The street is both busy and deserted. The corner is bounded by largely empty parking lots, one for a generic strip mall with off-price clothing stores, a big athletic shoe shop, and a discount makeup store. Another lot is for a national bank. Beyond that is a string of rubble-strewn lots left empty by demolitions. The landscape is a familiar one in Chicago, a city where entire neighborhoods can go underserved and overlooked for decades on end. Chronic disenfranchisement propels rates of poverty, trauma, and crime, too.

Belenge is uneasy. Idling there even for just a few minutes at seven in the morning, he feels unsafe after being confronted and intimidated by a group of boys just a week before. After a few minutes, Felix and Asani arrive. The two flank Belenge as they head for school. The walk to school takes thirty minutes and will go faster, he feels, with friends. The boys spend much of their time together, especially now that Belenge and his three younger siblings sleep next door at Felix's family's apartment most nights. During his first six months in Chicago, Belenge had been in charge of his younger siblings. His eldest brother had moved north to Wisconsin, where he had taken a job at a meatpacking facility outside of Green Bay. During those months, Belenge would pick up the three youngest from school and scrounge a dinner from whatever he found in the kitchen cabinets. Most of their food was donated by RefugeeOne or American co-sponsors.

Belenge isn't much of a cook. In Nyarugusu, his mother prepared their food. If he closes his eyes, Belenge can still smell the steamy aroma of her *fufu*. But she had died in 2014, and it was after that, that the role of parent fell to him, instead of to his father, Tobias. Although Tobias had lost other loved ones, his wife's death seemed to break him. Tobias would not have found the strength to move his family through the camps and to America if Belenge had not taken charge in Chicago, and if he didn't have the help of Felix's mother, his family would have broken into more pieces, too.

Once a small group gathers, Belenge and the others make their way south on Clark Street. An arterial street, Clark cuts directly through the Rogers Park neighborhood. The traffic moves much faster on Clark than on the neighboring residential streets, but at 7 a.m., the street has barely come to life. The multitude of taquerias, the mechanics' garages, and storefront law offices are still quiet. Only the Mexican panaderias, the aromas of fresh chamuco and concha wafting from them, have their doors open to passersby. Though Belenge and his crew could have ridden the Clark Street bus to Sullivan, it costs 75¢ per ride with discount cards provided by the school. The cumulative cost proves prohibitively expensive. Plus, Belenge prefers the fresh air. It's a welcome contrast to sitting inside stuffy, fluorescent classrooms where the temperature fluctuates between boiling hot and ice cold.

A few blocks from Sullivan, he passes the McDonald's on the west side of Clark Street. There's always a long line of cars waiting in the drive-through. Belenge can still recall the first time he stepped inside a McDonald's. Standing in front of the cashier, neck craned upward, Belenge froze. Before coming to Chicago, Belenge knew little about America and the information he did possess stemmed mostly from movies and music. As a result, Belenge's impression of American culture was formed by songs like 50 Cent's single "In da Club" and testosterone-fueled movies like *Rambo* and *Commando*. They left him with a narrow, often problematic, understanding of his new country, and none of the action movies included a wall of monitors filled with a tiled pattern of what looked like the same image: a hamburger and fries. Belenge ate his first-ever hamburger at the cafeteria at Senn High School, but it was presented to him without choice. How was he supposed to know the difference between the array of images at the restaurant? Even now, despite some practice, Belenge cannot decipher the chain's offerings. If asked, he keeps his order simple and to the point: hamburger.

This morning, the group passes McDonald's just before 7:30 a.m. If the boys pick up their pace, they can still make it to Sullivan for the free breakfast. Belenge and his friends are among the 90 percent of Sullivan students whose family incomes are low enough to qualify them for free or reduced-cost school meals. Usually, the boys arrive minutes before one of the cafeteria women rolls their mobile cart back toward the industrial kitchen. Belenge doesn't care much for the free breakfast. It usually comes with a limp, lukewarm Eggo waffle or English muffin paired with fruit and small carton of milk. In any case, Belenge prefers not to eat during the school day. He reasons that the more he eats, the hungrier he gets. In Nyarugusu, where food was always in short supply, Belenge would eat only one midday meal. He's grown accustomed to going hours on end without food.

Belenge's first class is English, his favorite. He's taken a liking to his teacher, Annmarie Handley. After that first week of waiting in the library while the school worked on his schedule, Belenge was placed in Annmarie's English language learner 1-B class. That section was tailored to students who speak very little English. Annmarie's classroom sits directly across from the library and about a hundred yards from the front doors. Even if Belenge arrives late to school, he can go from door to chair in seconds.

Sullivan is an old school, and in Annmarie's classroom the vintage school desks are made from blonde wood and sturdy metal legs. The seating chart that Annmarie gave to everyone on the first day put Belenge between two Rohingya classmates. When Annmarie asks the students to work in groups, Belenge communicates with these neighbors through the Google Translate app. The classroom is covered in flags and posters from countries all over the world. When Belenge first walked in, he immediately spotted the blue, green, and black stripes of Tanzania as well as the red, yellow, and green of the Congolese flag.

The school day passes slowly. When the bell rings at 3:04 p.m., Belenge rushes out the door. He plants himself just beyond the school's front steps. He knows he won't be allowed to stand here for long. Antoine Livingston, the dean of students at Sullivan, never lets students linger. Belenge stands on the sidewalk where his classmates gather in clusters. Just a few feet away, a group of girls, their hijabs an array of primary colors, climb into a car parked on the opposite side of the street. Mariah walks by and nods to the girls. She's cordial, but less than friendly. Up the block, several students make their way toward Devon Avenue. Shahina, and her closest friend, Aishah, are among them. The boys walk with a pronounced strut, exaggerated by their loose, topstitched jeans and low-hanging backpacks, while Shahina and Aishah shuffle behind, their arms linked.

While students newer to America tend to stick together,

and to their native languages, those who have lived in Chicago longer boast broader groups of friends. One Syrian junior, a star of the wrestling team, mills around with his teammates, a crew made up of a mix of refugee and American-born students. The boys huddle around a cell phone that plays a YouTube compilation of wrestling hip throws. Impressed by the athlete's acumen, the boys release a collective howl. A few feet over, a senior, whose unofficial uniform is a denim jacket, well-worn T-shirt, and frayed but fitted jeans, holds his guitar as he chats with his bandmates. He arrived in Chicago four years ago after fleeing Myanmar when the military tried to recruit his father and older brother as battlefield porters in the country's civil war. He laughs with Lauren, a Black American senior with short, tight curls and a warm, mezzo voice. Lauren participates in a variety of school clubs: Math, Newspaper, Magic the Gathering, Cooking, and the National Honor Society among others. The school rock band, though, despite the complicated web of crushes and broken hearts, remains her favorite. As a self-described outsider, Lauren finds that the band gives her a sense of confidence and place. Plus, she likes that the group counts refugee and immigrant students among its members. She chose Sullivan over better ranked selective-enrollment high schools because of the diversity. Behind Lauren, Alejandro, who always heads directly home, keeps his head down as he slips past a group of boys huddling at the corner. They exchange handshakes with guys Belenge doesn't recognize. Antoine Livingston's commanding baritone directs the boys, "Keep it moving, guys."

Belenge smells a coming rain in the air. He doesn't mind. Getting a little wet in hard-paved Chicago hardly compares to suffering the wet, gooey sludge brought by a heavy rainfall in Nyarugusu. When Felix and Asani arrive at the sidewalk's edge, Belenge hurries them along.

"Where have you been?" he asks in Swahili, agitated. "Let's go."

When the boys land at the Birchwood Avenue Apartments, they smell *sombe*, a cassava-leaf stew that is cooked with palm oil, eggplants, and peanuts. Children, some barefoot, others in oversized shoes, run from room to room. Toys and stuffed animals dot the floor, but they aren't always the favorite playthings. There are small balls of tinfoil and cloth that the children love to toss back and forth across the room. The tinny sounds of Tanzanian pop music playing from one cell phone speaker clashes with the loud canned laughter of Mr. Bean coming from another. Mama Sakina, the family and neighborhood matriarch, stands in the small kitchen hovered over the stove. Her turquoise zebra print and orange and red Kitenge cloth brightens the room. Her four-month-old baby, strapped against her back, bounces while she rolls cornmeal for *fufu* the Congolese way.

Felix and Belenge greet Mama Sakina politely, then retreat

to their bedroom. Plopping themselves down on the bed, they each cue up a FIFA game on their phones. For all the distractions America can offer, nothing matches the enthusiasm for soccer the boys brought with them. Soccer was, and remains, their Hollywood, baseball, football, and basketball all in one. In the digital versions, Felix always plays Real Madrid while Belenge prefers Arsenal. For Belenge, no one stands up to German player Mesut Özil. The two boys have a committed rivalry, though Belenge knows Felix remains the better player. The two play for the rest of the afternoon.

At 6 p.m., Felix gets a phone call from Esengo, his friend and fellow Congolese refugee. Can Felix help him with a pencil portrait for his art class? Felix is a skilled and disciplined artist. He spends entire days working on his portraiture. Felix's drawings remind Belenge of photographs. On Instagram, where Felix posts his work, he gets dozens of comments filled with fire and heart emojis.

Felix leaves for Esengo's apartment. The walk north will take him fifteen minutes. Belenge pauses the FIFA game and switches over to WhatsApp, the messaging platform preferred by the Africans he stays in touch with. He scrolls through a series of recent conversations. Belenge, a clotheshorse, likes to share photographs of his outfits. In one, Belenge pairs a white tuxedo jacket with black lapels and a white bowtie with a pair of marbled black-and-white cowboy boots. It's a low-angle power shot with Belenge staring down on the lens with a serious, tight frown. In another, he wears a fire-engine-red suit atop faux suede penny loafers accented by gold medallions. He stares down at the sidewalk, his head casting a shadow beneath him. One such photo showed Belenge after he broke his leg during an indoor volleyball game his first winter in Chicago. He asked everyone who entered his hospital room to take his picture. He wanted "all of Africa" to see him in the American hospital on an American hospital bed, leg propped and wrapped in tidy plaster.

Belenge spends the next two hours in the bedroom texting with a rotation of teenage girls whom he met online. He likes to flirt. He sends them episodes from the YouTube comedy show, *Mafundi*, about a plumber with big dreams starring one of Belenge's favorite young Kenyan actors, Jaymondy. He will also send love songs by Bongo Flava Tanzanian pop singer Diamond Platnumz. His favorite song, "The One," a profession of love, is also one of Platnumz most popular. He might also share Platnumz's song "Marry You," which he recorded with Neyo, the American singer known for his sweet, dulcet singing. Belenge, who sings in his church choir, has sung the song so many times he has it memorized. Maybe one day he'll sing it to a girl himself.

Just past 9 p.m., Felix returns home. Belenge sees his friend is frustrated.

"Esengo wasn't home," Felix says in Swahili, plopping himself into a chair. "I waited for two hours. He never came back."

Felix explains that he called Esengo when he arrived at his

friend's apartment. Esengo's sister had let Felix in. He was wet from walking in the rain. When Esengo answered the phone he told Felix that he was headed to Walgreens because his father asked him to get some juice. The pharmacy was only a few blocks from Esengo's apartment, so Felix figured it wouldn't take longer than fifteen minutes.

"Maybe he went somewhere else," suggests Belenge.

"I don't know. Maybe."

Later that night, as the boys begin to drift in and out of sleep, Felix's phone buzzes. He holds it up to his face examining the number. When he answers, Belenge can't quite decipher his friend's expression in the glow of his phone screen. Felix is quiet and stoic and doesn't emote much.

"Felix, this is Joseph, Esengo's father," Belenge hears the man explain in Swahili. "Have you seen Esengo? I haven't heard from him since I sent him to the store earlier today."

"No, I haven't," says Felix. "You should call the police. Say you lost someone. Describe maybe what clothes he was wearing and how tall he is. Tell them he's been gone all night. Maybe they can help."

Belenge sits up. He feels pangs of fear punching against his chest. Like Felix, Belenge learned from teachers at Sullivan that calling 911 was the first step in an emergency. He can hear Joseph crying.

"Esengo has never done anything like this before," he says.

"Don't cry," Felix says, trying to reassure him. "The police can be a big help. They can help find Esengo."

Belenge's entire body tells him something terrible has happened to Esengo.

A little over a week ago, when Belenge was walking his usual route home, a group of boys, who he recognized from Sullivan, surrounded him just before crossing onto Clark Street. One of the boys, barely taller than Belenge, started speaking to him in English. Belenge froze. He wasn't used to talking with his American-born classmates. The sophomore rarely interacted with classmates outside of the ELL population. In school, new refugee students only mixed with the rest of the school population in a select number of classes: art, gym, and music. There, activities like volleying a ball and learning to play a simple song offered a bridge for Belenge. Outside of those spaces, however, Belenge had trouble tracking conversations in English.

While Belenge couldn't understand the boys' words, he recognized the threatening tone. Belenge, who had his bike with him, gripped the handlebars as the group inched closer. Lifting his bike so it stood straight up on the back wheel, Belenge started shouting at them in Swahili. The gesture startled the boys just enough that Belenge managed to push his way between two of the boys and pedal the rest of the way home.

The following day at Sullivan, Belenge noticed one of the

same boys glaring at him from across the lunchroom. Belenge asked one of the school's security staff stationed at the doors if he could leave and go to the library. The man told him he needed a pass to leave the lunchroom before the period ended. Belenge understood, but he didn't have a pass. He returned to his table, sliding onto the attached thin blue bench. He pulled out his phone and didn't look up again until he heard the bell ring.

A few days later, Asani told Belenge that he and Esengo had been chased after school. Asani reported to his older brother that the two had been walking through Touhy Park when they were approached by four boys. Esengo, who spoke more English than Asani, confronted them. Then Esengo started to run. He only made it half a block before one of the boys grabbed him and clocked him in the face. But before the boy could land a second punch, Esengo managed to scramble away. By that point, Asani was running, too. Asani didn't stop running until he reached Mama Sakina's apartment on Birchwood Avenue.

The two incidents scared the brothers. But more than a week had passed since they were approached. Belenge figured the worst was behind him. But now, Belenge feels certain Esengo's disappearance is related.

Just past midnight. Felix gets another call. This time, it's Esengo's younger sister. By now, everyone has emerged from their bedrooms. Several neighbors, some clad in their pajamas, others still in their uniforms from their late-night shifts, have come over and stationed themselves around the living room.

"We found Esengo," she says over speakerphone. Her brother had been found at St. Francis Hospital in Evanston. He'd been shot.

Mama Sakina, on the couch cradling her baby, cries out.

Esengo's sister continues to explain that Esengo cannot speak. A bullet had collapsed his left lung. They'll have to wait for more information.

3
OCTOBER

Matt Fasana

Matt Fasana, Sullivan's assistant principal, arrives at school earlier than usual on Monday morning, October 16. Friday's shooting has left him with a pit in his stomach. He spent the weekend turning over the news, replaying the scene in his mind.

The forty-year-old had been sitting on his couch when he received a text from Chad on the night of October 13. He had just queued up the NBC drama, *This Is Us*, when his phone dinged.

One of our students has been shot. Living. Critical condition.

"Shit," Matt said, the word slipping out.

"What's wrong?" his wife asked, looking out from the kitchen where she was preparing her sugar-free, gluten-free, and what Matt considers "fun-free" lunch for the following day.

"One of our kids got shot."

"Shit."

Matt's cell phone dinged again. Another text from Chad.

The student's name is Esengo.

———

New information about the shooting has trickled in over the last forty-eight hours. According to a police report generated in the days following the shooting, fifteen-year-old Esengo emerged from the Walgreens pharmacy on Friday evening and noticed two young men standing in front of the store entrance. When the two boys called out to Esengo, he ran. He sprinted through the gangway and zigzagged through the neighborhood. As he turned into a nearby alley, one boy fired several rounds of 9-millimeter bullets. One of them struck Esengo in the back, piercing his upper-left scapula and lung. With blood beginning to soak through his multiple layers, Esengo managed to run to a busy street corner where he collapsed on the sidewalk. A woman standing outside the nearby Pockets Express noticed the boy fall. When she approached him, he looked up at the stranger.

"Help," he whispered, barely audible.

When the emergency medical technicians brought Esengo to St. Francis Hospital, a small pool of blood remained on the corner where he fell. At the hospital, the boy was listed as in critical condition. His left lung had collapsed. Indeed, doctors at the first emergency room that received him transferred him to a bigger, tertiary care hospital that handles harder cases. There, he was sent immediately into surgery where they removed blood from his lungs and the bullet from his upper-left back. After surgery, Esengo was reported in critical, but stable, condition.

When the detectives questioned Esengo at the hospital, he

wrote his responses on paper as he struggled to speak. Before he was shot, Esengo moved with an air of confidence. He was not intimidated by the crowded hallways or classmates who towered over him. He was stubborn and headstrong and often played leader among his friends. But as he lay in the sterile, bright hospital room, pain, fear, and confusion took hold.

At the hospital, everything Esengo reported was filtered through translators. When Esengo's telling eventually reached Matt, one piece of information particularly alarmed the assistant principal: Esengo claimed he was beat up by a group of Sullivan students just a few days before he was shot.

Pushing back in his office chair, Matt pulls up an email from Chad. The note, which Chad sent late the previous evening, outlines an After Action Review, or AAR. Chad learned this technique, a planning and discussion model used by the military in the wake of a destabilizing event—a bombing, for example—while working at Harper High School on the city's South Side. At Harper, gun violence permeated the school. The email outlines the basic facts of the event and Chad's short- and long-term plans to address it:

Student Review: Esengo, a Congolese refugee and freshman at Sullivan High School.
Crisis Incident: On Friday, October 13. Shot at Ridge and Touhy.

Condition of Victim: Esengo is currently being treated at Ann and Robert H. Lurie Children's Hospital for a collapsed lung.

The plan includes sending Sarah and Josh, the social worker at Sullivan who works with refugees and their families, to visit Sullivan's ELL classrooms where they are to discuss the shooting with students. Matt and Antoine Livingston are to help the Chicago Police Department with its investigation.

In recent years, Rogers Park, like much of the city, has turned into a complicated mix of block-level gang territories run by young men who have splintered off from the long-standing "super" gangs such as Gangster Disciples and Vice Lords. Kids who have spent their lives navigating the city have intimate knowledge of shifting gang activity. Like all neighborhood schools, Sullivan has students who affiliate with local gangs. Passing periods in the hallways include handshakes and hand symbols, but these are intricate, complicated codes difficult to decipher at first pass. Such gestures also exist among a sea of private languages that unfold inside Sullivan. Each time the bell rings, students stream into the hallways. Boys race toward the cafeteria as they tug on one another's backpacks. Young couples find hallway nooks where they whisper private messages in each other's ears. Class comedians loudly quote snippets from viral videos and employ creative jabs to poke fun at their teachers. Friends challenge one another to impromptu flossing and Benny Whip dance competitions while others pose for photos, each one meticulously edited to blurred-pore perfection. All while Sullivan's six full-time security staff belt out "Get to class" over the crowds. How is it then, Matt wonders, that refugee teenagers, new to the country and culture, are getting pulled into a violent web?

Later in the morning, a detective from the Chicago Police Department arrives at Sullivan. Tall with blonde hair, she stands inside the school metal detectors beside a security guard who sits at the front desk. She wears a black Chicago Police Department vest with blue jeans. It's never good when a detective shows up at the doors of a school. She's arrived from the hospital where she interviewed Esengo. Matt suggests they talk in the ELL office in the library.

Once there, she tells Matt what she knows: Esengo was likely shot near Ridge and Touhy Avenues, and Esengo gave descriptions of two black men, one tall and the other short. The detective also tells Matt she knows Esengo was attacked earlier in the week, and she believes the shooting could be the result of gang recruitment gone awry. The meeting is brief. Before the detective leaves, she tells Matt she'll be in touch.

Elsewhere in the building, Sarah and Josh visit Esengo's classes. Josh has come up with a simple, scripted version of the events.

"Esengo is alive," he tells the students. "We don't know

what happened to him. He is in the hospital. We are doing everything we can to support him and his family and all of you. And if anyone wants to come talk to me, please do so."

One student raises his hand, sheepishly. "I didn't know this happened in America," he says. Another asks if she can visit Esengo in the hospital. The news has sent a shockwave through the room. It's not an easy message for Sarah and Josh to deliver. How do you tell a group of students, some of whom have witnessed friends shot and killed, and others who have fled war zones, that violence besets their new home, a place that promised sanctuary and safety? Sarah and Josh stick to the script. But they know the students have plenty of trauma to read into it.

Asani

Asani, who is lanky with a gentle gaze, and Samuel, a shy freshman with round cheeks, arrive in the ELL office in the back of the library on Wednesday afternoon. The small room, cluttered with uniforms, bins of school supplies, headphones, and shelves filled with old textbooks, is out of sight, but wondrous things can emerge from it. Sarah refers to the room as the ELL "womb." Sarah settles into her desk chair at the end of a table. Matt sits beside her while Josh plops down next to the boys. Asani sits quietly, barely moving. Both he and Samuel grew up in Nyarugusu, a place where, rather than protect the refugees in the camp, police often demanded bribes—money, sex—to keep from hounding them. For the boys, police were an equal threat to gangs.

This is the first time Asani has left Mama Sakina's home since Friday evening. As Mama Sakina put it just a few nights earlier, Asani's father, Tobias, and their fellow Congolese refugees came to America for a safer life. But now, they no longer feel safe.

When the detective arrives, she comes with a colleague. The two introduce themselves to Asani and Samuel. The interview cannot start before a translator shows up on the phone. Several still moments later, an accented voice greets the room over the speaker and the questioning begins.

The interview unfolds at a glacial pace. It's slow in both languages. The detectives ask for basic details of the day that Esengo was beat up. The translator, whose voice is muffled by a bad connection, poses the question to the boys. Asani starts. He speaks quickly, barely pausing for breath. His answers verge on manic. He explains, in Swahili, that two weeks ago, Esengo was approached by a group of four boys. Esengo exchanged a few words in English with them, but Asani did not understand what was said. The boys then lunged at Esengo and he began to run. Soon, one of them caught Esengo and punched him in the face. He only got in a few hits before Esengo managed to scramble away. Before the translator explains, Samuel interrupts. He shakes his head and offers his own version of events. When the translator speaks to the adults in the room, he tells them the boys do not agree on when Esengo was beat up, nor where it happened.

The conversation does not get easier from there. The boys continue to interrupt each other, and while the translator attempts to keep up, he struggles to keep their answers straight. It takes almost an hour for the detectives to establish Esengo's route home from school. According to a neighborhood gang map, Esengo's path home crossed through three different gang territories: the blocks surrounding Sullivan High School are claimed by PBG, or the Pooh Bear Gang, a sct of Gangster Disciple members named for the fifteen-year-old rapper Pooh Bear who was murdered in Rogers Park in January 2012. On Ashland, Esengo crossed through a several-block radius where Ashland Vikings, a mostly Puerto Rican gang, runs its operation. Closest to Esengo's apartment building is an area known as "the jungle," a large swath of blocks run by Loyalty Over Cash, or Loc City, another offshoot of Gangster Disciples, locked in a nine-year war with PBG. In Asani's version of events, Esengo was attacked in Touhy Park, an area that falls just within Loc City territory. But the fact does not address why Esengo was targeted in the first place.

The detectives push ahead. One of them pulls out a set of pictures that Matt reluctantly printed earlier in the week. The images, without names, depict every male student at Sullivan. The detective's request had irked Matt, but the notion that the shooter could be inside the school compelled him to comply.

Matt's clunky machinery, however, printed the images so dark that the students' faces look barely visible and not always distinguishable. They also show the Congolese boys another set of images depicting individuals—teenagers and adults—who the Chicago Police Department has identified as active gang members. The line-up is hardly precise or blind. The detectives still ask Asani and Samuel if they can identify anyone. The 3:04 p.m. bell signals the end of the school day, but in the "womb" the sound is faint. The boys' day isn't over yet.

Asani and Samuel take their time with the pictures. They hold each image up to the light, shifting the pages from side to side. Different angles illuminate unique contours. The boys study the faces, consulting with one another in Swahili. They eventually identify two individuals, both Sullivan students, who they believe they saw the day Esengo was assaulted.

The interview ends just past 4:30 p.m., and the school is mostly empty. The detective offers to drive both boys home. They accept. The incident has left them terrified of walking through Rogers Park.

Matt follows the boys out. He can't help but absorb some of that fear, though he only has to walk a hundred feet to his car, which sits in the staff parking lot. As he makes his way there, his mind returns to a detail from earlier in the morning: midway through the meeting, both Asani and Samuel were visibly flustered. They had tried, unsuccessfully, to describe the moments before Esengo was punched. In an effort to clarify the details, Josh asked the boys to draw a picture of the scene. Samuel took charge and drew four stick figures in a diamond shape just below a fifth figure representing Esengo. He then drew an arrow pointing to the figure closest to Esengo and wrote the word "shooter" above it. Matt wonders how Samuel, who was not present when Esengo was shot, would know who shot his friend.

Sarah Quintenz

Shaking the news of the shooting proves difficult, but Sarah must shift her focus. Life inside Sullivan pushes forward. Sitting toward the center of the large, communal table in the library, her shoulders slightly hunched over her laptop computer, Sarah kicks off the agenda for the afternoon meeting. The first two weeks of October have come and gone, and Halloween decorations now hang throughout the building. The school gym is particularly spooky, thanks to a spread of Party City decorations, including string spiderwebs, giant plastic spiders, and a pin-the-hat-on-the-witch game. Perhaps most fearsome is the regular appearance of mice, which seem to have claimed the ELL office as their den. Josh and Danny Rizk spent a recent afternoon Googling how to trap the tiny creatures. One search suggests using Lactaid or peppermint sticks as poison. Another lays out instructions on duct-taping a hole. So far, however, the mice have evaded capture.

This afternoon's gathering marks another weekly discussion that Sarah has introduced in her new role as chair of the expanded ELL department. Sarah spent her summer break building up the department. Now she oversees an eleven-person staff and consults with another three who teach classes that include both ELL students and others. Collectively, the group works with over three hundred students, nearly half the school population. And there are lots of meetings.

Sarah starts with the good news. The department finally has its own printer. "We waited four years and we got it," Sarah tells the group of ten sitting around the table. "This is a big deal for us."

Sarah explains that she's working with Friends of Sullivan, a volunteer group of alumni and neighbors, on a Thanksgiving dinner. ELL is not all about language learning. Sarah firmly believes that students learn better when they feel a connection to American traditions. The Thanksgiving dinner is meant to bring together refugee students, alumni, and community members to share their traditions.

"So, can I ask a non-PC question?" one teacher asks. "Is this Thanksgiving dinner to teach kids about Thanksgiving or for us to show up for politicians and get donations?"

"Uh, neither," Sarah responds. "It's about Thanksgiving before all the killing and disease. Like, the sharing of culture and the Native Americans teaching the pilgrims how to live safely." This history is fiction, but it presents a version of America Sarah hopes to offer her refugee students.

Helping students feel welcome and safe has long stood at the center of Sarah's own pedagogy. During her time in the classroom, Sarah adjusted almost every lesson to make them relatable for refugee students. She once edited a standard reading exercise about visiting a laundromat to one that asked students to detail how they cleaned their clothes in their home countries. Or the country they fled, or the refugee camps they lived in. The students dug in, comparing stories of white shirts, dirty walls, and seeing underwear on the line. No matter the lesson, her goal was to help students feel confident and know that their traditions were just as valuable as what was outlined on the page.

Student safety has been a particular concern for Sarah and her staff, since Esengo was shot. Earlier in the month, Josh addressed the shooting through a series of role-play scenarios with students. In one, Danny jumped out of an alley as the students walked down the street. The lesson, Josh told the students, was to "stay away from danger." In another, Josh mindlessly walked into a street intersection while wearing headphones. As he stood there, another staff member drove through the intersection leaning on the car horn. The lesson? "Stay aware."

For Josh, planning lessons on city dangers must include elements of fun for students, so that his efforts don't retraumatize kids whose families may have been jumped, robbed, threatened, or worse before they arrived in the United States.

Sarah tells everyone that the Thanksgiving plans are still

shaping up. They have to work out the details, like where they can find a halal turkey and how to gin up some media attention. Just then a group of boys wanders through the door, their eyes glued to their phones.

"Hey, guys, you have to go somewhere else," Sarah says, turning toward them. They don't respond. "The library is closed," she continues, raising her voice louder. "Goodbye!" Looking up, the boys smile and leave. "Love you!" Sarah calls after them.

Sarah then turns to the biggest agenda item: writing a new ELL curriculum.

"In the last three years, we have been working on cleaning up our reputation," she says. "We've been building our program, and now we want to design cross-curricular units and focus on what we want to teach."

When Sarah first stepped into her role as chair of the ELL program four years ago, the department adopted what is known as the "cohort" model: ELL students travel together throughout the day, not just to English but to all core classes, where they receive language support. The idea was to keep students with similar English-language skills in the same classes. But new conflicts around the world created new crops of students, and what worked for Nepalese students didn't always work for Syrian kids. Building a curriculum that both addressed the basic needs of students, and remained nimble for changing demographics, would be a serious undertaking. Sarah enlisted the help of a lecturer at the School of Education at Loyola University, one of the city's big Catholic schools that serves thousands of first- and second-generation students from families who had to learn the ropes. Loyola is nearby, so must grapple with the same concerns, too. It's a place where Catholic kids from Latin America and Eastern Europe walk side-by-side with kids in turbans and hijabs. In some ways, Loyola is a bigger version of Sullivan, and a place where many of Sarah's students could thrive if Sullivan does its job right.

Sarah instructs everyone to cue up a worksheet she's written on Google Drive. She's outlined questions such as "Who are our students?"; "What do we want them to learn?"; "What are their biggest challenges?" But at its core, the exercise works to answer one crucial question: What does it mean to offer a refugee student their best chance for a good life in America?

The question Sarah and her staff cannot answer, however, is how severely the political tides against new immigrants will impact Sullivan High School's hundred-year-old purpose. Or whether Washington's public distaste for refugees will deny the city and nation of a group of young people made to survive and, with the school's help, thrive.

Chad Adams

Chad leans against the podium at the front of the room packed with Rogers Park community members, most of whom are longtime Chicagoans of every ilk who have come to advocate for their newest neighbors. The meeting, which Chad and

Rogers Park Alderman Joe Moore lead together, is a response to the outpouring of concerned, often seething, emails from neighborhood residents. The alderman's office suggested a meeting where community members could voice their concerns. He titled the event "Support Refugees Resisting Gangs."

Chad wears a button-down shirt under his navy-blue Sullivan track jacket. The former suited the solemnity of the proceedings and the latter dialed it down. The most urgent questions of the hour—how and why the shooting happened—will be hard to answer. The principal knows that anyone can be a victim. When he worked at Harper High School on the South Side of the city, Chad saw how gun violence traumatized students and their families. He lost count of the number of meetings with parents and neighbors who have wanted answers. He's heard over and over how gangs appeal to his students. All kids want to fit in, and for many, gang culture promises community and security. It often appeals to the most vulnerable and those who are outsiders. Refugee students are often both unprotected and unfamiliar. At Sullivan, Chad has watched as refugee boys—some from the Congo, others from Myanmar—begin to emulate the styles and cadences of some of their American classmates. Sometimes they don't even know the meaning of the lingo or the gestures they're trying on; more than anything, they try to belong. In any case, it signals to gangs that they have a way in. Chad always told himself he needs to expect calls like the one he got after Esengo's shooting.

From the podium, Chad nods to acknowledge a woman in the front row.

"So, my question is, you said you wished the family of the boy who was shot had reached out to you earlier, and I guess I'm wondering, what could you have done if they did?"

Chad's answer reflects that he understands the sense of panic among students and their families, and it also asserts the school's role as one of the students' protectors. The last thing he wants is for parents to think their children are less safe in school than out of school.

"Hearing from the family would have allowed us to do a little investigation, and make sure it's not one of our kids," responds Chad. "It would allow us to get a head start. We could have asked about who beat him up, what they looked like . . . We didn't have any of that information." Chad pauses. "I don't blame the kid for not telling us. The family didn't know to tell the school. But if we don't know, we can't do anything."

A man toward the back of the room stands up. "The bottom line is a young man ended up getting shot, so what could have been worse than that?"

A staff member from Joe Moore's office steps in. She explains this is precisely why she set up this meeting: her hope is to connect those working with refugee families with the Sullivan staff. Chad can feel the temperature rise.

"I can give everyone my card," Chad says from the podium. "I'll make sure you have my contact information."

"I volunteer with a Syrian family and they've got little kids.

I'm wondering does recruitment start at a young age and are there any ideas for little kids?" one woman asks.

"I'm sure it starts early," Chad responds without any condescension. "But I don't know what age exactly."

Just then, a slight man toward the front of the room stands up. "My name is Pastor Jim Larkin, Christ Church," he tells the room. "We have ten Congolese students attending Sullivan and gang recruitment usually starts around age twelve. What happens when you're recruited is you get beat up, and [after that] it usually turns into a five-year commitment. You have to go to meetings and pay dues. They say, uh, 'Once a King, always a King.'"

A voice from the other side of the room adds to the mix. "We also have to be aware that there are a number of African kids who are actually in a gang," he says. "They speak Swahili. Some are Rwandan, okay. I think we gotta be careful that we don't say they are totally, you know, American kids sucking in African refugee kids." He pauses. "And lastly, how come the police are not at this meeting?"

Next, a Congolese man, clutching his shoulder bag against his stomach, chimes in from the back of the room. "My name is John and I work for RefugeeOne. I think this is so difficult for parents coming from Africa. There are cultural issues here and children start going through the school system and they want to adjust and be like other American teenagers. This is hard for parents because they do not speak the language and they do not understand American culture."

"That's one of the reasons we asked all of you to be here," Chad continues. "Education should start at age four. I don't know what it should look like, but I know it should look something like what we're doing here. We're listening to kids and talking about what they see in their neighborhoods. We ask them what they see and if anyone has approached them. That sort of thing."

"So, it sounds like you're talking about gangs targeting kids because of being a refugee," one woman says, without raising her hand. "I was wondering if there's a pattern for recruitment in terms of certain ethnic groups or certain countries of origin?"

"You know, all kinds of kids are targets," Chad responds. "Especially ones who walk home by themselves because that's sort of a sign that you might not have a friend yet in this country, or in this neighborhood. . . . We try to build a sense of family here. But if you haven't found your way yet, you're going to be susceptible."

Matt Fasana

More than two weeks have passed since Esengo was shot, and little progress has been made in the investigation. After Asani and Samuel identified two potential suspects from the afternoon Esengo was beaten, Matt asked Antoine Livingston to interview the students in question. Antoine is the primary disciplinarian at Sullivan. He is built like a big-bodied linebacker—he played the position at Eastern Illinois University—and speaks in a deep baritone that projects from his chest. When Antoine pulled both boys into his office, they each admitted, remorsefully, to assaulting a Congolese refugee. They explained it had been playful bullying gone too far. But after showing them images of the new Congolese students, the boys identified Belenge as their victim, not Esengo. Belenge had also been harassed in the days leading up to the shooting. Matt reported this news to the detective. If true, this meant it was still a mystery which boys followed and beat Esengo.

Overall, the past two weeks have proven relatively quiet at school. No fights or signs of violence. The days are noticeably shorter and the wind cooler. A smattering of posters, all of them printed on standard paper, advertise candidates for homecoming queen. In one, a young woman stands with her hands on her hips and chest pushed outwards. In another, a girl is photoshopped against a background of diamonds, her mouth open as she smiles and laughs into the camera. The dance and game have passed, but the ephemera remain. Attendance has been good, including that of the American-born students implicated by the Congolese refugee boys. Because of this, Matt feels certain that the Congolese boys were confused. He finds it improbable that a violent perpetrator would return to school and keep his attendance up. Antoine, however, remains less certain.

Growing up in the Robert Taylor Homes, a now-demolished housing structure that was racially, and economically, separated from Chicago's traditional neighborhoods, Antoine was familiar with feeling isolated from the city around him. As a kid, he kept close tabs on the gangs who ran the area around his apartment complex. Everyone did. The Gangster Disciples and the Vice Lords each had their corner. Still, Antoine knew little of what lay beyond the boundaries of the neighborhood. Always large for his age, Antoine earned a scholarship to Leo High School, a Catholic school for boys, where he played football. He still credits that scholarship as his ticket out of the projects. For those who stayed, the line between gang culture and regular neighborhood ran thin. Some were born into the gangs, others joined because it made them feel safe. There were also those who joined up to try and claw their way to a different fate. Still others, compelled by violence, simply had no choice.

Antoine knows there are gangs inside Sullivan. He knows that gangs try to grow and recruit by any means necessary. If that sounds like how militias act in the war zones many of Sullivan's refugee families flee from, Antoine recognizes it. Chicago's tougher projects and the world's tougher conflict zones share some of the rules he grew up knowing. Now, every day after school, Antoine stands on the concrete front steps of the school building. With his arms at his side, and a Bluetooth headpiece in his ear, he watches. For the past several months, he's noticed a group of neighborhood boys who gather at the north end of the block. The group never approaches the building, but Antoine keeps tabs on which students greet the group with elaborate handshakes, the kinds with extra twists and turns. Those handshake greetings raise a red flag. They are, very literally, signs of potential threats looming around Sullivan High School.

Angalia Bianca

Angalia Bianca rings the doorbell to Mama Sakina and her husband Elombe's apartment on Birchwood Avenue, and waits for someone to buzz her in. Though there's a slight breeze, the temperature is warm for late October. Bianca—everyone calls her that—removes her jacket to reveal a bright orange shirt with the word "staff" written across the back. She's also in jeans, and combat boots, pretty much her usual weekday wear. Bianca has a small, black teardrop tattoo drawn between her sunken blue eyes and sharp cheekbones. Under bright light, her heavy brows cast her eyes in near complete shadow. Bianca has spent most of her life working the streets. She now works at Cure Violence, an organization that employs former gang members to build relationships with current gang members. The goal is to intervene in disputes that are likely to lead to retaliatory acts of violence and to stop, or reverse, deadly cycles of retribution. She's here to offer her help to the Congolese community.

Soon, a small boy comes running toward the door. He's

barefooted. Gloria Walsh, one of the family's co-sponsors, a group of volunteers who pool their resources to help new American families establish themselves in their new home, follows behind the boy.

"He doesn't have any shoes?" Bianca asks.

"They're just used to not wearing shoes," Gloria says with a nervous laugh. "He does have shoes."

Bianca follows the boy and Gloria up the stairs to the second-floor apartment.

As they approach the door, she spots several children's shoes piled just outside on the floor. Inside, a group waits around the dining room table. Bianca feels the fear in the room. Gloria introduces Bianca to Mama Sakina and Elombe. Tobias and Pastor Jim are also present, as well as another three women, two of whom are volunteer co-sponsors. Another one is a counselor from the resettlement agency RefugeeOne.

The meeting cannot begin before Felix, Mama Sakina and Elombe's eldest son, arrives. Felix's English is by far the most fluent among the boys in the family. Before settling into her seat, Bianca asks to use the toilet. When she pulls open the door, she notices that the bathroom is nearly empty. A soap bar has been worn down to a tiny sliver now stuck to the rim of the bathtub. A blue shower curtain, its bottom blackened with mildew, is pushed back toward a rusted showerhead, and a single sheet of toilet paper remains on the roll.

Before she joined Cure Violence, Bianca was a Latin King

for twenty-seven years. She has been arrested more than 125 times, convicted of twenty-six felonies, and spent more than twelve years in prisons. She has seen more dead bodies—many of them belonging to teenagers—than she has the stomach to recall. At sixty, Bianca is no stranger to hardship. That's one of the reasons she was asked to help the Congolese community in the wake of the shooting.

But now, standing in Mama Sakina's bathroom, Bianca's heart breaks. *These families have fled horrific, unimaginable conditions,* she thinks to herself. *They've come with nothing, and now they have to deal with* this *bullshit? No money even for soap, and one sheet of toilet paper for the whole family. How are they supposed to feel protected in their new country when they are so poor?* A wave of sadness hits her. She takes a breath, then returns to the living room. Felix now sits with his parents at the table; Belenge, Asani, and Felix's younger brother crowd together on the small couch. Pastor Jim speaks first.

"Okay, we are here to talk about how we can keep you safe," he says in a firm tone, looking at the boys. "The kids need to return to school."

Elombe, speaking through Felix, responds. "I do not want to send my children back to that school."

"How can we figure this out? What's the update with the district?" continues Pastor Jim, referring to his attempt earlier in the month to pull the boys from Sullivan and transfer them to the nearby Mather High School. "Can we bus them there?"

One of the women at the table explains that it won't be easy to transfer the boys. For one, they do not live in the Mather school district, and for another, Mather is already well over capacity. She also suggests that transferring the boys to another school won't necessarily alleviate their fears. But Pastor Jim remains unconvinced.

"We need to figure this out," he says, repeating himself. "We need to get them to another school."

"I need my children protected," Elombe reiterates. "They cannot go back to this school. I want to leave Chicago. I do not feel safe here."

"We are doing our best to keep everyone safe," says Gloria, responding directly to Elombe.

"I want answers."

The conversation proceeds in circles. Eventually, Bianca speaks up.

"Can I speak with the children directly?" she asks Elombe. He agrees. Shifting her chair toward the couch, her back now to those sitting at the table, Bianca looks directly at the boys. "First of all, I want to tell you that you can completely trust me, I'm on your side," she says. "I want to help you. I'm not going to ask you to tell me things that could put you more in danger, that's not what I do, but I want to ask you, is this happening after school or in the school?"

Belenge responds in a near-whisper. "Both."

"Do you know who approached you? Can you give me any idea, so I know who to talk to?"

"PBG," Belenge says. And then, as though panicked, he says it again. "PBG. PBG." That, of course, is the Pooh Bear Gang.

Belenge's answer confirms what Bianca already believed: PBG was likely responsible for shooting Esengo. Before coming to the meeting today, Bianca visited one of her contacts inside PBG, who, at twenty-two, was considered old by street standards. He told her the shooter was likely one of the "young shorties," the fourteen- and fifteen-year-old guys who want to prove themselves and tend to be reckless along the way. Though Bianca didn't get a specific name, she had anticipated that PBG members were the culprits, and that it was the young shorties who were the attackers. She was so sure that she had already delivered her message to them face-to-face a few days earlier: *This can't happen. Are you guys so desperate that you're now recruiting people from the Congo? What the fuck is wrong with you? If you keep this shit up, don't ever call me again. Ever! Don't call me from jail. Don't call me when your baby needs formula. Don't call me when you need a ride. Never call my number again. If you don't cut this shit out, I'm done trying to help.*

Bianca leans toward the boys, as though to emphasize her next point. "Okay," she says, "I want you to know, my cell phone is always on. You can call me anytime. If you're in the school, you can call me if you feel threatened, I will drop everything, walk out, and come and get you."

The boys nod, though it's unclear to Bianca if they understand what she's offering. She then turns her chair back toward the adults sitting around the table. "I want you to know, I was able to talk with the high-risk youth in the neighborhood. I want to ensure they leave these children, and all children from the Congo, alone."

"Well, if they take the bus to school, how are you going to protect them?" Pastor Jim asks, his tone now verging on condescension. "Can you go on the bus with them?"

Bianca knows she can't ever truly guarantee safety. "Well, no, sir," she responds, steadily. "But I will continue to work with the gangs to make sure they stay away from the boys. I will continue to follow up."

Pastor Jim shakes his head. He remains perturbed. The only solution, as he sees it, will be to pull the boys out of Sullivan High School for good. That will certainly have consequences for the boys, but it will also affect the school and its ability to serve immigrants and refugees. This is a big deal for everyone.

By the end of October, the perpetrator and his friend remain unknown to the police and the school administration. But for Esengo and his family, the result of the investigation has no impact on their choice. They have made up their minds to leave the city for good. They feel there is a remaining threat inside Sullivan, one that could erupt at any time. They aren't going to be victims again. After spending a week at the hospital, Esengo and his family pack their clothes and whatever belongings they can fit in their suitcases, and board a Greyhound bus to Iowa.

4

NOVEMBER

Belenge

Belenge has hardly left Mama Sakina's apartment in nearly a month. If he does leave, it's to pray at Christ Church in Albany Park where Jim Larkin is pastor. Housed in a nondescript box of tan brick, the church fits the new built-for-economy style that dominated the neighborhood in the 1960s. The giant white cross on its exterior hints that the building is more than a small factory. So does the facade that reads Christ Church: A Church for All People, which, with its mix of Congolese refugees, Central and South American migrants, and long-term locals seems true.

The first Congolese refugee to worship at Pastor Jim Larkin's church walked through the doors in 2014. He asked if he could pray. Soon, he became a regular at Christ Church, and started to bring other Congolese refugees who were resettled in Chicago to Sunday services. Faith and Christian fellowship are strong in Chicago's Congolese community, and Christ Church quickly became a central space for the growing number of Congolese refugees arriving in the city. By 2016, nearly half of the three hundred congregants at Christ Church were Congolese. Since many spoke little to no English, Pastor Jim introduced a second Sunday service that was led by a Congolese pastor in Swahili. After the Sunday sermons, the church hosted a simple meal of chicken, rice, salad, and *fufu* for the families. Breaking bread together strengthened the church community. Pastor Jim liked to imagine that the Sunday ritual allowed the Congolese families to feel like they were back in their homeland. Over time, the families began sharing their stories with the pastor. It amazed him that, despite the hardship they described—waiting four hours for water at refugee camps, eating spoiled rice, suffering miscarriages due to illness and malnutrition—these families continued to put so much trust in God. They inspired him and serving them was a calling he embraced wholeheartedly.

The chapel inside is decorated sparingly with maroon carpet, white-painted brick, and wood pews, but it's a warm hub of spirited worship and play and full of African fashions. It now feels like a second home for Belenge. When fear begins to take him prisoner—a sensation that has occurred frequently since mid-October—Belenge can hold on to scenes from Sunday choir when congregants sing traditional Swahili songs and hymns and end the morning with home-cooked Congolese meals made by the women and girls of the church.

But soon, Belenge's community at the church will shrink, because even this home is infected with fear after the shooting. Belenge hasn't heard much local news about the investigation. For Belenge, who cannot yet read much English, the only information he receives comes from Mama Sakina, who gets word from her American co-sponsors.

Esengo hasn't reported much, either. Belenge didn't get a chance to say goodbye to his friend before he moved to Iowa. Many Congolese refugees remain in flight mode, even after arriving in the United States. Leaving comes naturally when your sense of home is transient across town, across countries, and across continents. What's a move a few hundred miles to Iowa for safety when a ten-thousand-mile move from Congo's violence lands families in a city among kids with guns? Recently, Belenge heard his father speak about leaving Chicago. Work is hard to come by, rents prove expensive, and now the city, which was supposed to offer safety and security, threatens.

In mid-November, Mama Sakina relays to Belenge that Gloria Walsh, who has come to the house every day since the shooting, has offered her support. Gloria, retired with no children of her own, has embraced the role of the hyper-vigilant counselor. A former human resources representative, Gloria considers it a responsibility to protect Belenge and the broader Congolese refugee community. Her co-sponsor group has offered several Congolese families help navigating the complexities of life in their new country. She gives rides to Belenge when he needs to leave the house. She also takes Mama Sakina to her doctor's appointments and to a far-flung grocery store that sells cassava roots in bulk. She helped Belenge's father, Tobias, land a job at the Bruss Company where he works through the night packing meat into Styrofoam containers. All told, Gloria spends upwards of forty hours each week volunteering.

Now, Gloria explains that she worked with RefugeeOne to set up a meeting with Sullivan teachers and administrators where she intends to argue for something that both she and Pastor Jim agree on: that Belenge and the Congolese boys must leave Sullivan as soon as possible.

When Gloria pulls up outside Mama Sakina's apartment on a Thursday morning, Belenge is not yet dressed. He'd lost track of time. Gloria, patient and unshakable, waits in the front living room while Belenge puts on his suit. He's chosen the sky-blue number that he normally saves for Sunday church services. The two-piece functions as a kind of armor for Belenge.

In the car, Belenge remains quiet in the back seat. Gloria, who normally communicates with Belenge through the Google Translate app, turns on WBEZ, the local NPR affiliate station. Waves of troubling news fill the airwaves. Some reports detail the continuing devastation of Hurricane Maria in Puerto Rico while others summarize emerging information from a recent mass shooting in Las Vegas, the deadliest in U.S. history. News of Harvey Weinstein's abuse of power and sexual misconduct has dominated the airwaves lately. But Belenge remains mostly unaware of the headlines and Gloria does not translate. Belenge's father, Tobias, who Gloria said must also come to the meeting, stares silently out the passenger window.

The three arrive at Sullivan. A security staffer tells them to wait in the library. Stepping into the hallway causes Belenge's entire body to tighten. His breath quickens and his legs seem to move only in slow motion, as though pushing through wet, heavy earth. Power has so long been used to thwart, not help, them. Even the blue suit magic can't quicken Belenge's step. Belenge trails Gloria who walks toward the library.

They settle into the small metal chairs at the end of the long, rectangular table in the center of the room. They wait as the room fills with Sullivan staff. When the table is near full, Sarah begins the meeting, but she soon turns it over to Antoine Livingston, who explains that the school still has not identified the boys who beat up Esengo before the boy was shot. He asks Belenge to help in the matter. That confuses Belenge. As though reading his mind, Gloria, who has asserted herself as Belenge's advocate, tries to divert the request. She tells Antoine she believes two of the Congolese boys had already been questioned. Nonetheless, Belenge tries to answer.

Through a translator, Belenge explains that in the weeks before Esengo was shot, two boys tripped him and confronted him in the cafeteria during lunch and again on the school steps at the end of the day. He explains that he does not want to return to Sullivan because he fears the boys will target him next, especially because he's already been bullied. Intentionally, or not, Belenge is a step ahead of Gloria. By talking, and heightening the threat against him, he ups the chances of being transferred out of Sullivan.

"Hold on," says Sarah, confused. "I thought this meeting was supposed to be about how to help Belenge, who feels he's failing in school?"

Gloria contradicts the notion. She explains that she hopes this meeting will help identify a solution that will allow the boys to feel safe again. In her opinion, she explains, transferring the boys to the nearby Mather High School is likely the best option. Tobias remains quiet.

Matt stiffens across the table. Mather is hardly a better sanctuary for refugee students, some of whom transferred from Mather because they found the school unwelcoming or overwhelming. Sullivan is the school with programs in place to acclimate students like Belenge and to work with their families. The fact of this meeting exhibits as much. At Mather, Belenge could lose the support Matt can muster for him. He also knows that losing Belenge and Asani to Mather High School could quickly spiral into the loss of upwards of ten refugee students, who would all lose that support. The Congolese refugee community is tight knit. If one family pulls their kids from Sullivan High School, others will surely follow. If such events do indeed unfold, the impact on Sullivan could be grim. The economy of Chicago Public Schools (CPS) operates by a simple calculus: more students means more money. Ten students leaving could mean losing as much as $60,000 from the school budget, roughly equal to a first-year teacher's salary. The fragility of the refugee students' world can infect even the best supports they have in the United States.

Tobias looks up. His eyes, normally puffy and glassy from sleeplessness, alcohol, or the potent cocktail of the two, are sharp. He pushes his chair back from the table and stands up. His small frame looks even smaller under his oversized winter jacket. He raises his hands, which are marked by deep grooves and calluses formed from years working as a carpenter and long hours packing slabs of meat.

"No one here is Belenge's father," he fumes in Swahili. "I am his father and he needs to return to school tomorrow. If he is going to die, it is in the hands of God."

Tobias's outburst leaves Belenge in shock. The boy cups his hands over his face and begins to cry. For much of Belenge's life, Tobias has remained aloof. Though Tobias rarely speaks about the past, Belenge understands that his father lost a part of himself when he left the Congo in 1996. For the Bembe, the connection to the soil of one's homeland is spiritual as well as physical. The earth is guarded by the spirits of ancestors, in Swahili commonly called *mizimu wa mababu*, who ensure the generations remain tied to their land. Belenge knows few details about the brutality Tobias witnessed. But he knows his father well enough to understand that he would never have left the Congo if it wasn't a matter of life or death, and the fact that all but one of Tobias's surviving children have never touched

Congolese soil weighs heavy on him. Tobias himself will never feel whole until he returns to the Congo. Now Tobias spends much of his time trying to forget these traumas. He drinks them away; he prays them away. He buries them deep beneath the surface. Or, he tries to fit them into God's plan, which can feed his rage more. It's a rare occasion that Tobias's ghosts morph into explosive, violent anger. When that happens, Belenge retreats. But here, at Sullivan, Belenge cannot hide.

Tobias walks toward the door of the library, threatening to leave. Before he pulls the door open, someone asks him to sit back down. He complies but remains irate.

"I will not sign a form for Belenge to change schools," he says, adding that he recognizes the school's care for his son. "If Belenge is not back at Sullivan tomorrow, he cannot live in my house. I came to America to give him an education. He can go back to Africa if he does not come back to school. Belenge is a baby; he is not a man."

This is final. The group around the table spends the last few minutes of the meeting discussing logistics. A neighborhood watch group has offered to drive the Congolese boys to and from school each day. Josh plans to work with Belenge on his anxiety. Sarah will discuss Belenge's missed work with his teachers. Everyone agrees that Belenge will return to Sullivan the following Monday. The school, they promise him, will do everything they can to support him and make him feel safe. And be safe.

Back in the car, Gloria offers to drop Tobias at work. He's picked up a daytime shift at the meatpacking factory where he normally works nights. When she pulls into the parking lot at the Bruss Company, Tobias turns to her and thanks her. He then opens the car door and disappears inside the long low-slung factory. Gloria drives Belenge back to Mama Sakina's apartment. As soon as they enter the building, Belenge can smell wafts of garlic, onion, and hot oil. The smell relaxes him. He's home.

Thanksgiving

Sitting in the back room of the library, Sarah opens a chocolate chip cookie from the 7-Eleven that stands just a few blocks north of Sullivan. The cookie is half her favorite lunch menu: Diet Coke and sugar. Leaning back in her chair, Sarah looks at her phone. There's a text message from a teacher. One of her new Rohingya students has locked herself in the bathroom and she hasn't been able to coax her out. She knows Sarah is the woman for the job and has reached out in hopes that Sarah can retrieve the girl and bring her back to class.

Keyed up on caffeine, Sarah marches across the hall and pushes open the swinging wood door to the bathroom. The bathroom is the unofficial lounge for refugee girls. But the Rohingya girl is there to hide, perhaps because she's been treated badly or feels out of place, or because there's been some trigger at the school that caused her to freak out.

Just inside the door, several girls chatter in Arabic as they crowd around a small mirror mounted on the wall. Their pink and purple backpacks have been piled into the corner as the girls reapply their eyeliner and lipstick and adjust their headwear. They appear unbothered by the dank air and smell of sewage. Sarah greets them as she passes and makes her way down the bathroom aisle, looking for a door that remains latched shut. When she reaches it, she knocks on the stall. The girl, just over five feet tall, who arrived with a recent wave of Rohingya refugees, opens the door. Sarah doesn't know the details of her story. She often knows little about the new students who come her way, and even the students Sarah knows well keep their secrets buried. As well as this, there are the regular high school anxieties like gossip and sidelong glances that can be enough to send someone into the bathroom. She may have arrived in Chicago by way of Malaysia, where she would have been isolated from a school system that does not permit Rohingya children to attend. If she came from one of the overcrowded settlements along Bangladesh's Cox's Bazar, a thin strip of land that now precariously holds three hundred thousand Rohingya refugees, she likely lived in thatched bamboo housing, and spent her days working to keep a tiny square of land from sinking in the mud. Sarah can only guess. But today is the school's Thanksgiving dinner, and she takes her cue from the day.

"Honey, you can't hide in the bathroom," says Sarah. "When

you don't come to class, you can't learn from your peers and they can't learn from you. And they want you to be around."

The girl looks up at Sarah, so she continues. "Don't hide in the bathroom," she says. "If you need to hide, hide in the library."

The Thanksgiving holiday holds special meaning for Sarah. Growing up, Sarah moved around a lot. By the time she was fourteen, she had lived in five cities including London. Her stepfather served as a marine and retired from the navy when Sarah's family moved to Chicago. In Chicago, Sarah's mother worked as a public middle school teacher for twenty years. Sarah considers Chicago home because it's where she and her three siblings threw out her stereo boxes. Throughout the years, no matter where Sarah and her family landed, her mother always invited those without Thanksgiving plans to their family table.

After Sarah returns the Rohingya girl to class, she heads back to the library where she still has half a cookie to eat. When she walks into the office, students fill nearly every chair. The group, who call Sarah "Mom," congregate here at the same time every day. For many, eating lunch in this small, cramped space is the closest they come to having a family meal, as many of the jobs available to new refugees—cleaning airplanes at O'Hare International Airport or late housekeeping shifts at hotels, for example—require working through the evening and into the night. Sarah knows this, and encourages students to join in.

Today, the group includes Alejandro, who's watching a soccer game in Germany while slowly making his way through a bag of Doritos. Alejandro spends more time in the ELL office than anywhere else in the school. Much of the time, he sits, watching a game or scrolling through YouTube videos. Sometimes, he simply lays his head on the table and sleeps. The room is a haven. Next to Alejandro sits a freshman girl who occupies herself taking selfies. Danny Rizk walks in, laptop under his arm and Nalgene water bottle in hand, and plunks down onto his seat. The motion causes the back of the chair to kiss the carpet. He recites the lyrics to Kendrick Lamar's "Element" to himself, but loud enough for the room to hear. After several rounds of "I don't give a fuck," Fatima Peters, who works as an ELL reading tutor, looks up from her laptop when she hears the word "goddamn."

"Danny! You are sitting next to a former Catholic school teacher; you can't say GD."

"My cousin is in that gang," the freshman girl adds. "GD. I like to add K to the end, and he's like, don't disrespect me like that." She goes on to narrate a long, meandering story about her family's gang affiliations. She explains that her ex-boyfriend was killed by a rival gang last spring and she was in the hospital room when he was pronounced dead. She offers the story with little emotion or flair. When she finishes, she returns to her phone.

Sarah is only partially listening. She's looking over a string of text messages. Her attention is required on the other side of the building where she's deputized ELL students to put up decorations for the Thanksgiving feast.

Sarah quickens her pace as she walks toward the first-floor community room. She began introducing her students to American Thanksgiving the second year she taught ELL at Sullivan. Sarah saw how the mythology of Thanksgiving paralleled the journey of her students, and when she shared America's foundational story with them, she asked the refugee students to share their own stories, too. Now she hopes to expand that exchange to the broader neighborhood and Sullivan community.

But when she reaches the community room, Sarah stops in the doorway.

"Shit," she says, holding her hand up to cover her mouth and nose. The room stinks. "Did something die in here?"

The stench is a potent contrast to the giddy students waiting to festoon the room with streamers.

But dealing with the smell will have to come later. Sarah first needs the students to put up the decorations so she can cross the task off her list. Sarah passes out yellow, orange, and red paper streamers and boxes filled with paper leaves and bags full of glitter to a group of students who sit waiting for instructions.

"You like this?" she asks, rhetorically. "CPS trash decorations? You guys have to figure out how to make this look nice. I can tell you the streamers should stretch across the ceiling."

Speaking in a jumble of languages, the students reach into the boxes and pull out supplies. They start with the streamers. A Rohingya boy scrunches a pile together in an attempt to make a less-than-elegant centerpiece for a table.

"No!" shouts an Afghani girl grabbing the material from him. She unravels the mess of paper and carefully twists each strand around another, as though shaping a giant, multi-colored paper Twizzler. The boy looks on with curiosity. Without saying a word, the girl hands him one end and points to the wall.

"There," she says. "Put there." She walks the other end of the streamer to the opposite wall. She tells a friend to grab some tape. Once both sides are taped to the wall, the two, now working as a unit, pick up another set of streamers and repeat the process.

A few minutes later, Matt walks in. "It smells like something died in here," he says, holding his fingers to his nose. "We used to have that problem in my old school. You never forget that smell."

He turns to Sarah who, along with several plastic-glove-wearing students assembles ten place settings at each table.

"I think we're at thirty-eight languages, right?" he asks her. He's spent the morning preparing his opening remarks for the dinner. "This CPS count says we have thirty-five countries, but that can't be right. Shouldn't we have the same number of countries and languages?"

"No," answers Sarah, "because you could be from Burma and speak Burmese or Rohingya depending on your background."

He nods and jots down the correction on his paper.

Over the course of the next hour, the room begins to come together. Five twisted streamers hang over the tables, giving the room a boost of color. But despite the addition of color and sparkle, the room still reeks.

Sarah deputizes Danny and Josh to handle the smell.

"Could be the possum who lives in the basement?" asks Danny, walking around the room in order to identify if the smell becomes more potent in certain spots.

"No, I think Pocco is still alive," says Josh. "There's also Chester the mouse from the library. Maybe he made his way over here and died."

The Sullivan building is filled with creatures living just out of sight. Many Chicago public schools, especially those housed in hundred-year-old buildings, struggle to keep rodents, vermin, and pests out of the building. But with a leaking roof and ramshackle gym with aging rafters, and a basement of warrens, Sullivan's animal kingdom thrives, and dies.

———

An hour before Sullivan's Thanksgiving is set to start, the community room has been transformed into a festive banquet hall. Each of the twelve round tables has loaves of homemade bread hollowed into cornucopias, all of them designed and baked by students under the guidance of a Rogers Park volunteer who taught the teens how to make them. Each cone is stuffed with symbolic bounty including chestnuts, a Western symbol of prosperity; tangerines, an Eastern symbol of luck; and Medjool dates, a holy fruit used to break the Ramadan fast and one that's mentioned twenty-two times in the Qur'an. Each cornucopia sits surrounded by hand-colored paper flags from Myanmar, Syria, Iraq, and Somalia, among other countries. The tables are dusted with glitter and the stink has thinned thanks to an army of fans and an assortment of Febreze products. In the hallway, long picnic tables have been set up for the spread of food. Paper pumpkins and pilgrims hang from the edges of the tables, and a handwritten sign that reads "Welcome to Sullivan Thanksgiving" is taped to the center.

Among the first to arrive is a community member—a drum-circle-leading, left-leaning Jew and Sullivan alum—with a giant roasted turkey. He tells Sarah he wasn't even sure a twenty-five-pound turkey would fit in his oven, but sure enough, it did. He's trailed by several other older Rogers Park residents who grew up in the neighborhood and attended Sullivan themselves. Sullivan's alumni network boasts over three hundred members, the bulk of whom graduated before 1970. Many of them are Jews, and children of Holocaust survivors, and to them, Sullivan was a place where strict teachers pushed them to success. It was also a place that made them street-smart. They're grateful, and they've come to pass their affection forward.

With each guest who arrives, the spread of food expands: Waldorf salad, cranberry sauce, tin trays full of roasted tomatoes, avocado and grapefruit salad, cornbread, a vat of mashed potatoes. Just before 7 p.m., students begin to filter in. Sarah asked each of the students to invite their parents, but she had little expectation that any would show. Some parents are deterred by the language barrier. Others have no school experience themselves, and even for those who have, they've been taught that home and school function as two distinct, separate worlds.

No students come with their parents in tow. Nearly all of them, however, carry a homemade dish prepared by their mothers. Despite their parents' absence, each family, no matter how little they have, has found a way to express their gratitude. One Syrian junior drops a massive plate of *maqlubeh*, an upside-down chicken and rice dish layered with roasted vegetables, almonds, and poultry. The dish, a stunning architectural feat, fills nearly a quarter of the table. A Somalian senior, dressed in a floor-length, flowing mustard dress with a matching hijab, carries a platter of *sambusas*, or fried stuffed dough pockets, and places them at the end of the table. Two Afghani siblings arrive with beef and chicken kabobs, both halal, paired with peanut sauce and sliced cucumbers.

Just before the dinner is set to begin, a group of Rohingya boys come running down the hall. One boy, a small junior who has become the de facto leader among the group, carries two plastic bags with him. Rushing up to the spread of food, he sets them down and pulls out two Styrofoam takeout containers. A nearby student asks him what's inside. The boy reports he bought the food from Ghareeb Nawaz, a fast-casual Pakistani restaurant, just a few blocks from Sullivan. The containers are filled with chicken biryani and mixed vegetables.

"No one will know the difference," he says with pride.

In all, the group of students and Sullivan alums lay out a lavish spread of dishes from four continents. The splendor here is a measure of the lengths the students' families go to when playing host, even if the school community room is a proxy for their tables at home. The gesture is particularly poignant given the scarcity that many families face at home.

Inside the community room, guests begin to take their seats. Sarah planned the evening with speakers and activities and the program is outlined on each table. First, Lauren, the Rogers Park native who has dressed up for the occasion and wears a striped black and white dress that flares out from the waist, kicks off the night. For Lauren, the night celebrates what she loves best about her neighborhood. Outside of school, Lauren can spend an entire day exploring the intersecting worlds of Rogers Park. From behemoth plates of spicy biryani from a local Indian joint to her favorite grocery store with fresh carnitas by the bag, Rogers Park has offered the senior a passport to the world. She's also learned patience. When Lauren was a kid, her closest friend was a neighbor who was first-generation Mexican American. The girl spoke Spanish at home and whenever Lauren visited for a playdate, she struggled to keep up with the conversation. That experience stuck. It gave her some small window into what she imagines her new refugee and immigrant classmates navigate every day.

"There are students here from all over the world," says Lauren, standing at the front of the room holding a microphone and notes in the same hand, while gesticulating with the other. "I know so much more about culture and life and about different places that I've never been to. Just coming to school one day is like taking a trip around the globe and I love that so much."

Next, the founder of a newly formed community group called Friends of Sullivan, who have helped organize the event for tonight, says a few words. He tells the room that Thanksgiving is the most wonderful American holiday and it's a pleasure to share the tradition with Chicago's newcomers. Next, Matt takes the microphone and offers some data on the students at Sullivan.

"We all have our elevator speech about where we work," he says, "and I don't talk test scores. We have thirty-eight languages spoken here. We have so many different cultures learning from each other. We have kids from the Southeast Side meeting students from Southeast Asia. And there are so few places where you can see these cultures meeting with each other."

Sarah walks to the front of the room. Originally, she hoped Alejandro would read his "I Am From" poem. Sarah asked several students to write such poems on that theme for the Thanksgiving event. Alejandro's was poignant and she wanted the other students to see that side of him. Alas, Alejandro's father broke his leg in a soccer game and called the senior to give him a ride from the field to the hospital. So now, Sarah stands up in the front of the room alone.

"Every year, I would do a lesson on Thanksgiving with my students," Sarah begins. "The Indians, they already lived here. They were the first Americans. They sat down for a feast with both groups bringing their dishes, their stories, and their traditions. I share this piece of America's history, a piece of my history, and ask my students to share their history. Because our history, our stories, our past, and our traditions make us who we are today. To the new Americans in the room, we old Americans welcome you and embrace you with open arms."

When Sarah finishes her introduction, she invites Alejandro's replacement, a Ghanaian student whom she's asked to read his own version of "I Am From." He quickly gets up from his seat and makes his way to the front. Without looking up at the audience, he nervously dives into his poem.

> I am from Ghana . . . We live a peaceful life and eat fufu, which is made from the plantain plant . . . Dreams are everywhere . . . I know we came here for a better education, but it still hurt because I miss my friends . . . Ghana is country well-known, full of gold . . . I believe my country will be powerful one day . . . Dreams are Everywhere

When he finishes reading the poem, the boy returns to his seat at a table toward the back of the room. He sits between an alum from the graduating class of 1965 and a Ugandan senior. He picks up his fork, stabs a piece of turkey meat, and relishes it.

The next morning, the library is once again alive with students. In the absence of programs and decorated tables, another kind of cultural exchange is at work. Ihina, a Nepalese senior with a penchant for dirty jokes and cutting observations, sits at the edge of a table.

"Where y'all from?" she asks, eyeing a group of boys in the corner.

"Syria," one of them answers.

"Shit," she says, stretching out the word for several seconds. "Syria? Your country is fucked up."

Danny looks up from his phone. "Ihina," he says, amused, "you're from Nepal."

"Shit, I know."

Josh Zepeda

Josh waits in the ELL office in the back of the library. He's cleared the room so he and Belenge can have some privacy for their first session. Belenge has been back at Sullivan for a few days, but he has yet to return to the classroom. Instead, the sophomore keeps to the library catching up on missed schoolwork. Belenge is allowed to remain in the library because the few times the boy stepped into the hallway during a passing period, he froze in fear. When he recounted the feeling, Josh suspected Belenge suffered from second-hand trauma, although in refugee students, first- and second-hand trauma often compound.

Josh knows that trauma is part of the cultural fabric inside Sullivan. As much as 75 percent of refugee youth experience some level of post-traumatic stress disorder. And for whatever trauma stems from students' experiences before arriving in the States, there's the additional trauma of resettlement and navigating life in America. Refugees qualify for Medicaid health coverage, which includes therapy and counseling for psychological trauma in Illinois, but the practices are foreign concepts to most refugees and few take advantage of the services.

Josh was raised by Mexican and Chilean immigrants, and hoped working as a school social worker at a massive school just north of Chicago that's neither urban nor suburban, but a combination of both, would connect him to first-generation Americans who may feel caught between two cultures. Josh himself experienced a similar tug-of-war growing up Latino in Libertyville, a mostly white, wealthy suburb of Chicago. But his work didn't pan out that way. Instead, nearly every student Josh worked with came from a wealthier, white family. Of the school's thirty-five hundred students, Josh had close to four hundred under his watch. Mariah was among them. At twenty-five, he found the load untenable. Josh quit his job in June.

He spent the summer contemplating a career change. He considered playing music full-time or going back to school. In August, Sarah called. Josh had met Sarah while doing an internship at Sullivan as part of his master's in social work. Though Josh's internship did not focus on refugee students, he found himself drawn to them. Sarah took note. When Sarah called to discuss a job, Josh, who was raised a devout Catholic, considered it a sign from God. Sullivan would be a second chance at this work.

When Belenge enters the small room, Josh encourages him to take a seat. He points to the chair next to him. Josh can clearly see how fear has seized Belenge. A goofy dancer and talented soccer player, Belenge never seemed uncomfortable in his body before the shooting on October 13. Now, he hunches his shoulders and keeps his head tilted toward the floor.

"We're going to work on some stuff to help you feel less scared," says Josh, speaking deliberately, slowing down his natural, enthusiastic pace. He pauses on the word "scared." Belenge doesn't appear to understand what Josh means. Josh pulls out his phone and types the word into Google Translate. *Hofu.* To ensure Belenge understands, Josh also mimes the emotion, widening his eyes and mouth and placing his hands on either cheek. Nonverbal communication holds equal importance in finding the right words. Belenge smiles, now understanding what Josh means. He nods. Josh then asks Belenge if he's feeling anxious. *Wasiwasi.* He tries to convey the feeling with his eyes, but the nuance is hard to communicate. Belenge doesn't seem to process the notion. Anxiety will be a tricky idea to communicate. Google Translate only goes so far. He'll return to that one.

Josh presses forward. He wants to teach Belenge how to calm himself down when he begins to feel paralyzed with fear.

"This is what you do when you feel *hofu* or *wasiwasi*," Josh continues.

Josh scoots toward the front of the chair and sits up straight. He takes a deep breath, exaggerating the sound. As he does so, he pulls his arms upward as though pushing air through his lungs. He looks at Belenge and nods at him, encouraging him to do the same. Belenge complies. They're communicating.

Josh holds out his hands and uses his fingers to count down from five. Once done, he begins to exhale slowly, constricting the back of his throat, and pushing the air out through his nose.

"Slowly," he says to Belenge, who mirrors Josh's movements. "*Polepole.*"

Josh repeats the breathing cycle several times. As he does, he watches Belenge and guides him. Can the boy feel air moving into his windpipe and down into his lungs? The rise and fall of his chest? Yes, again. Josh continues to take slow, deep breaths, squeezing his words in between. Once the two have practiced several rounds, Josh motions Belenge to stop. Josh wants to show the boy a second exercise he can practice while sitting in class. He tells Belenge that it will help him when he begins to feel tense. The word, however, is not as easy to translate, so Josh settles for nervous. *Neva.* He tells Belenge to stare at his toes. He should focus on his toes, then relax them. Next, he should direct his mind to his legs. Are they tense? Relax. *Pumzika.* Josh instructs Belenge to inch his way up his body until his every limb loosens. He instructs Belenge to practice the exercise. He watches as Belenge tries it out. He starts and stops several times, frustrated. Josh tells him to keep trying. It may feel silly, he says, but it will help. He urges Belenge to try.

Pulling himself forward on the chair, Belenge closes his eyes. He sucks in a long, deep breath and begins. He does it again. And again. He does it until it almost feels natural.

Sixth period is almost over and Josh can hear a group of Syrian boys begin to congregate. Belenge hears them, too. He loses focus. Today's session is over.

When the two meet the following week, Belenge performs the exercises with a little more ease. The week after that, he's even more relaxed. By the end of November, Belenge returns to the classroom.

TOBIAS

•

Belenge's father, Tobias, never spoke much about his home village
in Fizi, a territory in the South Kivu Province of the Democratic
Republic of Congo where his family's tribe, the Bembe people,
lived. When he did speak of Congo, Tobias offered one simple
belief: "Home is who you are and I am Congolese."

In Fizi, Tobias was born into a family of farmers. As the only
son among nine children, Tobias was taught the family trades:
harvesting tree nuts and carpentry. Like many Bembe families,
Tobias's relied on farming. The nutrient-rich soil was used to grow
rice, maize, groundnuts, beans, and bananas. By the time Tobias
married his first wife in the early 1980s, Congo was ruled by
a notorious kleptocrat, Mobutu Sese Seko, who had turned the
country into a mess of corruption. Across the country, healthcare
systems broke down and mortality rates pushed past emergency
thresholds. In eastern Congo, children accounted for more than
45 percent of deaths due to diseases like malaria, measles, and
malnutrition. Tobias and his family were not immune. Over the
course of their marriage, Tobias and his first wife had five children, all of whom died before age six. Not long after her fifth
child died, his wife fell ill and died in a local hospital.

Tobias married again in 1991. Three years later, the long-
standing conflict between the Hutus and the Tutsis—two African ethnic groups—in Rwanda, began to spill into the Congo.
In 1994, Hutus seized power and massacred eight hundred

thousand Rwandan people, mostly Tutsis. A Tutsi-led rebel army retaliated causing more than one million Hutus, including some who orchestrated the genocide, to flee to Congo. With an influx of Rwandan refugees spread across the eastern edge of Congo, the border areas, including Fizi, erupted in clashes around ethnicity and land ownership. Amidst the growing mayhem, rebel groups with access to firearms took hold of Bembe villages. Tobias, who believed the agitators to be Rwandan Tutsis, was forced inside his home as he watched militant squads burn homes and farms and round up young local boys to train them as soldiers. During the most violent stretches, Tobias and his family would flee to the rainforest and hide for days at a time. This pattern held for a year, but in 1995 Tobias's two eldest children were killed in a flare-up of violence. His second wife died less than a month later.

A year later, in 1996, Mobutu steadily lost grip of the country and was eventually overthrown during a coup staged by Laurent Kabila with the support of both the Rwandan and Ugandan governments. Once Kabila was in power, Rwanda invaded South Kivu, announcing it intended to crush Hutu militias on the Congolese side of the border. With little left for him in Fizi, Tobias fled with nothing except his two-year-old daughter strapped to his back. Some Bembe people fled for the mountains, but Tobias joined a group of hundreds as they ran toward the rainforest. When the group reached the forest, each family tied themselves to one another with rope, encouraging the young and athletic to lead the pack. Tobias, who traveled only with his young daughter, remained separated. He figured it would allow him to freely move among the mass of people.

It took Tobias more than ten days to walk more than 600 miles to Lake Tanganyika. The rainforest canopy provided shade and mangos, but the threat of death was ever present. Many around Tobias died from dehydration while others drowned in the fast-moving rivers. Some starved and hundreds were mowed down by roaming militia groups. Tobias only stopped to sleep and pull fruit from the trees and water from the ground. When he dug for water in the mud, he'd often have to scoop the liquid into his hands while stepping over half-buried bodies. He'd grown accustomed to death. The journey was hard on Tobias's young daughter. She cried often, her screams loud in Tobias's ear. Tobias serenaded her with lullabies his wife used to sing. One, a Christian song, soothed the toddler. Some days, he repeated the simple tune and lyrics until his voice went hoarse: *Now the home is burning the day, and your mother has gone to the farm, who is going to put out the fire? It's me, I'm the only one at home.*

When Tobias reached Lake Tanganyika, he was told to board a small fishing boat. He could see many such boats traveling across the lake, each one overcrowded and weighed down by passengers. The war had pushed hundreds of thousands of Congolese from their home country. The violence, which continued through the following decade, would eventually displace 4.5 million people and kill another two million. At the edge of the lake, Tobias watched several boats capsize before reaching the Tanzanian shore. Tobias, who did not know how to swim, held tightly to his daughter as he climbed onto the wooden boat. He was told it would take eight hours to cross the lake. He closed his eyes and prayed.

When Tobias reached the Tanzanian border, he was put on a bus and taken to the city of Kigoma where the newly formed UN Refugee Agency camp, Nyarugusu, had been constructed. The seventeen-square-mile camp, which was built to hold fifty thousand refugees, would eventually offer shelter to more than three times that many. At Nyarugusu, Tobias was given a white tent, the blue UNHCR logo printed on its side, which was plotted in a sea of tents, the string of white canvas bright against the red dirt. He was given one pan, one pot, five cups, and five plates. The UN officer also provided semolina flour, beans, and cassava root. This would be the same set of ingredients he would receive once each month during his twenty years inside Nyarugusu. Outside his tent, Tobias cooked over an open flame with wood he'd gather from the surrounding forest and water he'd pull from a well and boil in his pot. He'd eat once a day, in the late evening, to ensure his food lasted the month.

As more refugees arrived, an informal economy began to take shape. On Mondays and Fridays, residents from the dozens of internal villages would set up a large market where they sold flowers, fruit, and handcrafted goods. On one such occasion, Tobias spotted a young woman twenty years his junior who caught his eye. He proposed that same day. Within a year, the two had their first child. Belenge, their second of six, was born in 2000. When his sons were old enough, Tobias enlisted the boys to help him build a more permanent house on their land. By the time Belenge was a preteen, Tobias and his family lived in a one-room brick building big enough for three beds. Though there were several primary schools inside the camp, Belenge and his brothers spent most of their days playing soccer. On bright nights under a waxing moon, they'd gather with friends and listen to the rapper 50 Cent and flirt with neighborhood girls.

Life was steady inside Nyarugusu and Tobias never expected to leave. But in 2014, he and his family were selected to be resettled in Chicago. He had never heard of the city, but Tobias knew of the United States. He'd heard of a priest who'd moved there. But Tobias's wife, who was pregnant with twins, would never see America. Eight months before Tobias boarded an airplane for Chicago, his wife and both babies died after she suffered a septic embolism.

In August 2016, as Tobias looked around the massive airplane filled with refugee families, he thought the structure looked like a house. There was food and bathrooms—someone showed him how to use a flushing toilet—and blankets. Tobias buckled his seatbelt and settled into his seat. He hardly moved the entire flight. Looking out the window, Tobias watched the clouds float in the air. Behind them the sun rose, fell, and emerged again.

5

DECEMBER

Sarah Quintenz

Sarah stands outside of her office. She hugs a well-stuffed plastic garbage bag. She turns the bag upside down and a pile of clothes spills onto the table. Dozens of such bags have arrived at Sullivan High School after Sarah put out a call for donations for their Christmas drive for ELL students. Sarah surveys the room. Instead of books, a wall of shelves is now filled with sweatshirts, pants, plates, highball glasses, lotions, toy Santas, vases, and cooking utensils, which will fill her students' kitchens next year. Sarah's goal is to transform the library into an ad hoc storehouse where students and their families can choose from donations in the days leading up to the winter break. She calls it the "Q Mart."

Sarah started gathering donations her first year at Sullivan after she'd seen students skate across icy winter sidewalks in flip-flop sandals and others push against frigid winds in just thin sweatshirts. She started by asking her siblings, mother, and stepfather to contribute at their weekly Sunday dinners. She pressed them to give up old jackets or winter boots. From her family alone, Sarah managed to gather several bags' worth of clothes. She expanded her network in the following years, emailing Sullivan staff and asking friends to post on Facebook. Sarah would spend much of December collecting and carting everything from cell phone chargers to jewelry boxes to baby clothes back to Sullivan. Sarah's entreaty is now a holiday ritual of its own. And her family and friends somehow manage to dig up more stuff every year.

A few minutes after the fifth period bell rings, a flood of students pour into the library. They are trailed by Dirk Casto, an ELL teacher, with his etched face and wicked humor, who instructs the students to station themselves around the library. One girl from the Central African Republic spots a box full of cosmetics. She whispers to her three friends and the girls make a beeline toward it. They dive in. One pulls out a lavender-scented lotion. She pumps a glob onto her hand, delighting as the product hits her skin. She sniffs and smiles. She pumps several more globs and begins to coat her arms in the lotion. Another girl pulls out bath soaps. The third finds a Revlon eyeshadow palette. She pops open the face and arrays the colors in swatches on her inner wrist. Her friend finds a perfume bottle and spritzes in the air. The girls lean in and enjoy the aromatic mist, debating the identity of the scent. They agree it is some kind of flower.

Behind them, a group of boys gather around a small Bluetooth speaker. One of them syncs his phone and plays the Turkish pop megastar Yalin. One of the world's top-selling pop stars, Yalin doesn't have mainstream status in the United

States, though in 2007, he had a successful collaboration with Jamaican singer Shaggy. Yalin's songs are sung in Turkish and Arabic, and are odes to loves lost or out of reach. The boys, broad-shouldered and tall, drape their arms around each other and begin to dance in a circle. The circle grows as young men from the other side of the room run over to join in the dance. They sing along to the melody as they hop around, in an ever-expanding circle.

Sarah doesn't interrupt them. She's cultivated a sociable atmosphere in the library. Many refugee teens find themselves in a strange middle space: At home, they often care for both their younger siblings and parents, many of whom suffer from deep trauma and struggle to adjust to their new lives, while at school they can shed those expectations and act like kids. Sarah knows several of the dancing boys go from school to eight-hour shifts at work. One of them manages the frying station at the McDonald's a mile west of school. Another cooks on the line at a Palestinian-owned diner. Several deliver for Uber Eats, and a few work at a country club just north of the city.

When Sarah had her own classroom on the first floor, she approached the space in a similar way. She would begin every class with music and often share her favorite singers—Dave Matthews, Justin Bieber, G. Love, the Clancy Brothers—and sometimes play songs from the radio. But she'd also encourage students to bring their own music to class, which they'd play for one another on their phones. Sarah also decorated her room so it felt like a place where playfulness could thrive. She covered nearly every inch of wall with flags. She hung plastic globes from the lights. Sarah, who got pregnant the first week of her first year of teaching—a fact that makes her groan-laugh when it comes up—also put up posters of her young son with accompanying classroom rules. An image that depicted her toddler covered in ice cream, for example, said: "Clean up after yourself, your mother doesn't work here!" Another, which showed the boy floating in a swimming pool, read, "Don't be afraid to swim in the deep end."

The posters also prompted students to ask Sarah about her home life. She joked that she hated football because her ex-husband loved it. She told them her son knew all the words to the Johnny Cash song "Walk the Line" before he could read. Sometimes Sarah would write down quotes from her son—"Grammie and Grumpa want to know if you want to sleepover?" for example—and ask her students to infer his meaning and fix the grammar. One year, Sarah transcribed a birthday message from her mother that detailed the story of Sarah's birth. It went like this: *You were born during* The Quiet Man. *I went in during the fight scene and you were born during the love scene.* She then assigned her students the task of writing their own birth stories from their mothers' perspectives. The results left Sarah in stitches.

When students expressed concern about attending college, she told them about her older brother who never went and still paid his bills. He had his own business, she said. And a career in the military. But she also liked to use her brother to offer lessons in what not to do. For example: When you first get your license, don't take your parents' Ford Aerostar van and speed through leaf piles because they might billow up and set the car engine on fire. This is why Sarah plans to one day write a book titled *794 Lessons My Brother Never Learned*.

Back in the library, the song ends. Sarah steps in. "Okay, guys," she says motioning the boys to turn down the music. "The queen is talking. When the queen is talking, you listen, and I need everyone to start folding these clothes."

"It looks like Macy's in here right now," adds Dirk Casto as he folds a pile of clothes, "but it better look like Nordstrom's when we're done." He laughs to himself. The joke wasn't meant for the students.

As students scatter to different piles of clothes, a tall junior boy manages to shimmy his way over to the Bluetooth speaker. He brings up a YouTube playlist for Tanzanian pop singer Lava Lava. He decides on the hit single "Teja," a love song with an auto-tuned melody over a syncopated beat. The boy drapes a lavender coat over his shoulders and starts to bounce his knees and move his shoulders to the beat. Soon, he's dancing, his feet moving in an intricate line step. His friends recognize the steps and form a line around him. A sophomore boy films the scene for his Snapchat story. The Swahili song has a popular Arabic cover version. The kids connect in surprising ways, from a Turkish singer's performing in Arabic, or a Tanzanian star who's caught on in the Arab world.

"You're so beautiful," says the boy who's filming, teasing, but without mocking.

"Thank you," the dancing boy says as he spins in place, his lavender coat whipping against the air.

Across the room, a Rohingya boy has started his own fashion show. The sophomore has put on a bra over his shirt and traded his sneakers for pumps. He struts back and forth across the room, swiveling his hips from side to side and dipping his shoulder from left to right. Shahina and Aishah trail behind him. They giggle and shriek.

"You're crazy," laughs Shahina as the boy throws his head back and cackles. When he reaches the bookshelves, he stops and poses. Shahina trails the boy with her phone, documenting every moment. Within minutes, her friends across the city, Midwest, Myanmar, and Malaysia will get a taste of her hybrid world, where old and new traditions weave together inside Sullivan's walls. Shahina often uses her own platform to test the boundaries between the two. Her Instagram selfies showcase long, loose, dyed hair, which dusts her face as she purses her lips and pretends to kiss the camera. Her followers are used to these kinds of images.

But frolicking in Chicago can be incendiary back in the Muslim Southeast and South Asia, through which refugee families have passed. Traditional tolerance for cross-dressing is losing ground there, and in some places such as Malaysia and some provinces of Indonesia it is punishable under newly strict Sharia-based law. When girls from Myanmar, a country relatively tolerant to cross-dressing, pass around a video of a playful classmate, the borderless show broadcasts everywhere and who knows how the hijinks register where they're seen out of context. But for now, the laughter continues. After Shahina posts the video of her friend, she turns the camera on herself, layering her hairline with floppy, spotted dog ears.

Alejandro

Alejandro has been on edge for months. Slumped in his seat in the fifth row of the school auditorium, the senior, who hasn't removed his backpack, pulls out his phone. He's not particularly interested in the winter holiday concert, or what Sarah calls "mandatory fun." On stage, a Rwandan boy beats on the drums while a Syrian sophomore accompanies him on flute as a group of singers belt out Tom Petty's "Free Falling." Students across the auditorium film the show with their phones while staff, most of whom lean against the southern wall, sway slightly in place. Next up, a second group sings "Feliz Navidad." Alejandro looks up; he knows this one. The program continues with "Jingle Bell Rock" and "Auld Lang Syne." When Lauren steps up to the microphone, the room cheers. She may feel apart from her peers, but she is not without fans. The rest of the Sullivan rock band shuffle in behind her. Hardly a beat passes before the first notes of No Doubt's "Just a Girl" sizzle across the space. The senior singer is backed by the Burmese bassist and together their swells of sounds bring dozens of students to their feet. With each verse, Lauren seems to lean deeper into Gwen Stefani's righteous anger. It's a sharp contrast to her general soft demeanor, but the edge suits her. By the time she reaches the first chorus, she crescendos into a full belt. A handful of students shout-sing along with her. Alejandro, however, isn't so moved. He's back on his phone, absorbed by a FIFA highlight reel.

It's hard for the eighteen-year-old to lose himself in a school concert while he lives in limbo and waits to make his final appeal for asylum. Unlike refugees, who arrive in the United States with protected status and who are given green cards and a path to American citizenship after five years in the country, those like Alejandro, who seek asylum after reaching the U.S. border, must plead their case to an immigration judge. The judge, in turn, decides whether to grant the individual asylum or deport them back to their home country. For the last five years Alejandro's immigration status has been litigated repeatedly and there's another hearing at the end of the school year. The new Trump administration policies, which include increasing the number of ICE officers, prioritizing prosecution of immigrant offenses, and limiting privacy for unauthorized immigrants seeking status, put Alejandro on tenuous ground and anything he's involved in just might work against him.

A few days later, when Alejandro walks into the ELL library office looking for respite from the hallway and the noise in his head, the room is already full. In one corner, Mariah sits flanked by two boys. These two stick to the Iraqi sophomore like shark suckers. Next to Mariah, Josh encourages two Congolese girls to sign up for after-school activities. He walks them through a long list of options: guitar club, soccer, band, poetry club, volleyball. No matter what he suggests, the girls shake their heads no. The girls frustrate one of the social worker's chief missions, which is to get the refugee kids engaged outside of class. Socialization is key, the school believes, to the kids' successful integration and to their happiness over time. Josh can usually persuade everyone to do something, but the girls at the school can be a challenge. The boys play soccer and the team has made the school a kind of star. In 2016, a filmmaker produced a documentary about the immigrant team and their Albanian coach, himself a refugee. It offers a model for the kind of socialization Josh pushes for. "Life here is easier," says one player in the film. "People go to work, get money, but in Rwanda it's very tough to get a job . . . The way soccer helped me out is it connected me to people . . . It introduced me to people who will help me have a better future."

If Josh gets kids into the right activities, they can succeed at something they care about. That builds confidence and networks. Migert Baburi, the Albanian coach, believes that soccer, for instance, gives kids a way to win in a world that conspires against them. "That's a war on that field," he says in the film. "It's you against me . . . There aren't any tanks against these kids. There is no airplane throwing bombs at them. It's a way they can win, and they can win by will."

As for the two girls, their families often prefer that their extracurriculars center around their churches. At first. Josh will get them into choir, or other musical groups, but it may be in their second or third years. For now, the pair are steadfast and insist none of the offers interest them.

"You guys don't want to do nothing," Mariah says, watching the exchange as she eats a fatayer, or triangular breaded pie, stuffed with spinach and feta. The two girls look back at Mariah, confused, wondering, perhaps, why she cares. But there's little at Sullivan Mariah doesn't care about or weigh in on. If it galls her that the girls don't want to mix in with other students after school, she says so. That's her school spirit. She wants the school to work for everyone, and at the same time rebels against the rules herself. But she's a force and charismatic, too, so while she'll upbraid others, no students correct her.

Alejandro looks at Mariah as she speaks. His main goal during his free period is to be quiet and find quiet. He mostly keeps to himself. Growing up in Guatemala City, Alejandro learned that visibility never worked in his favor. MS 13 ran his neighborhood. Violence and death were endemic. The best way to survive was to remain inside, or, if he had to leave home, in the shadows.

In 2013, Alejandro arrived in Chicago to meet his father, who too had come to the United States a decade earlier. Though he had put twenty-eight hundred miles between those who hunted him in Guatemala City and himself, Alejandro has never felt totally at ease. Not only were the killings and other violent memories impossible to shake, gangs seemed to be everywhere in Chicago, too. When he started as a fresh-man at Mather High School, a modernist white brick building that housed more than 1,650 students, Alejandro felt invis-ible. He liked that. But when he came upon a group of boys smoking a joint in the bathroom, Alejandro was awakened to a world inside Mather. He started to see drugs all over the school. He noticed gang symbols on lockers and coded hand-shakes between boys in the hall. Though the gangs were new, he recognized the modes of communication. After just a few weeks at Mather, Alejandro told his father he wanted to trans-fer to another school.

Mariah's brashness intrigues Alejandro, but she's also a threat to his invisibility. The two often sit across from one another in the ELL office, but they rarely speak to each other. Every time Mariah comes in, she's fueled by a grievance she wants to air. Whether it's a friend who has wronged her or a teacher who annoys her, she always fills the room. Alejandro observes. He watches soccer on his phone. He is certain Mariah doesn't know his name. The fact doesn't bother him.

"What *is* that?" one of Mariah's admirers asks as she takes a second bite from the spinach pie.

"It's Middle Eastern food," Mariah responds, a little dismissively.

"It needs sauce. Is that wasabi?" he says, pointing to a bottle on the table. "I had wasabi once and I was in the bathroom for weeks." The boy sticks out his tongue.

Mariah offers the boy a forkful of pie. Alejandro looks down at his bag of Doritos. It's nothing to get excited about, but it fits his budget and fills him enough. He's never had Middle Eastern food. He tried takeout Chinese food for the first time after arriving in the United States, and he likes kung pao chicken. He's tried matzo ball soup and bagels. Alejandro's father works as a handyman at assisted living housing for religious Jews. Sometimes, when he helps out his father on the weekends, Alejandro eats lunch in their cafeteria. Not his favorite cuisine. He prefers Mexican food. Ever since his girlfriend, who is Mexican American, introduced him to spicy salsa roja and salsa verde, Alejandro has eaten tamales and tacos almost every day after school.

Watching Mariah eat her spinach pie, Alejandro wonders what it tastes like. But he doesn't like to ask women for favors. One of the first lessons Alejandro's father, Sergio, taught him when they reconnected four years ago was never let a woman pay for a meal. Alejandro doesn't ask for a bite.

At Sullivan, Alejandro landed in Sarah's English class. At first, he disliked Sarah. Her acerbic style doesn't work for everyone. She pushed her students by repeatedly asking them: *Are you dumb or are you learning English?* A refrain that Sarah first used when pointing to a poster of her toddler son. She said: "You are not dumb. He's dumb *and* he's learning English." And added, "You all know how to wipe your own butts, I hope."

Her point was that no one should mistake the student for slow because they didn't speak English. But while students' English proficiency was not a measure of their intelligence, they still had to speak the language in Chicago to be taken seriously. The expression became a classroom catchphrase. But Alejandro didn't buy it. He found Sarah's haranguing humiliating. She got under his skin. And one day Alejandro, who had managed to temper his anger, burst wide open.

Midway through class Alejandro made a snide remark under his breath.

"Knock it off, Alejandro," Sarah said from the front of the classroom.

"Shut the fuck up," Alejandro responded in Spanish.

Sarah turned away, prepared to let the comment slide. But then another student spoke up.

"Don't talk to her like that," the student responded to Alejandro in Spanish. "*You* shut the fuck up."

"Don't tell me what to do," Alejandro said, now more heated.

"She's the coolest teacher we have. Seriously, don't talk to her like that."

Both boys stood up from their chairs. Alejandro threw a punch. He was knocked down by a retaliatory blow. There was blood on the floor. Sarah yelled for Sullivan security guards, who ran from the front desk to her room within seconds.

A few days later, Sarah met with Alejandro's father. She

told Sergio his son was both acting out and clashing with others. Sergio explained that ever since Alejandro had arrived in the United States he'd been angry about everything. He was angry about leaving his mother and his friends. He was angry at his father, who had become a relative stranger in their years apart from one another. Sarah implored Sergio to spend more time with his son.

The fight was a turning point for Alejandro and Sarah. When Alejandro learned that Sarah hadn't told his father about the fight, he thanked her. After that, he started spending his lunch periods in Sarah's classroom. By spring, Alejandro ate every day with Sarah. The classroom that broke his patience was now his safe space. He not only ate lunch there, he came to maintain order at other times of the day, too. He helped keep the room neat and Sarah's work manageable. She joked to him that he was her Secret Service detail. If students came to her with questions when Sarah was engaged, Alejandro would intercept them. "Ms. Q. is busy right now," he'd say, "ask me."

Alejandro shared details about his new relationship. He chronicled his growing love for salsa and tamales and complained about teachers he'd come to dislike. He never, however, talked about his past. That changed when Sarah assigned Jorge Ramos's book *Dying to Cross*. Like many of her teaching units, Sarah hoped the book, which tells the stories of nineteen people who died inside a trailer truck that was meant to carry them from Latin America to Houston, Texas, would connect with students' own migration stories. The class spent one full month discussing the book and its themes. She had students present on different characters and stories. When the class reached the section in the book that detailed how migrants crossed over the Rio Grande to reach the U.S. border, Alejandro spoke up.

"I did that," he told Sarah and the class.

"You crossed a river?" Sarah asked, puzzled.

"I crossed *that* river."

Sarah pulled up a map on the overhead projector. She pointed to it.

"This same river? The Rio Grande? What was that like?"

"Really fucking scary."

These days, the ELL office remains one of the only places Alejandro finds community. He tried other groups, but nothing stuck. When he first started at Sullivan, he played on the soccer team. Alejandro was a strong player and leader; he was elected team captain his second year on the squad. While everything else was new in America, the rules, pace, and play of the game remained the same as in Guatemala. When the team took to the field, they weren't thinking about the people they'd left behind. Alejandro didn't focus on his precarious future. The world shrunk to the size of the field. He found comfort in that. But soccer also brought out his anger and competitive nature. A bad referee call would leave him fuming. And once triggered, Alejandro found it difficult to reel himself back in. So, after his sophomore year, he quit. He also tried going to church with his girlfriend and her family. They went every Sunday and always shared a family meal afterward. But Alejandro was turned off by how women dressed up for church. He thought the short skirts and low-cut tops looked like outfits meant for a dance club. He decided he'd prefer to pray at home. From then on, whenever anyone asked him what his church was, he told them, "My house."

Last month, as Alejandro prepared to make his second plea for asylum, he asked Sarah to write him a letter of support. In the days leading up to his November 9 court date, he spent almost every period in the library. He'd hole up in a corner and consult a stapled stack of papers. The document, a script of sorts, consisted of the forty questions of the intake questionnaire given to unaccompanied migrant children once they are brought into custody, as well as his answers. The questions, which are modeled after those on the I-589 form, the U.S. application for asylum, are meant to turn difficult, complex lives into well-shaped narratives. For Alejandro, the specifics of his escape from Guatemala were hard to recall. They have faded as he's built a life in Chicago. But his lawyers told him he had to do his best to memorize his answers. They told him that the judge would try to catch any discrepancies. When Alejandro felt overwhelmed, he'd turn to Sarah who would always carve out time to talk.

———

Less than forty-eight hours before he was due in court on November 9, Alejandro received a phone call. It was his father, Sergio. He explained that the lawyers had called and told him that Alejandro's court date was being pushed back. The court was behind on its cases and it didn't have time to hear Alejandro's. He'd have to wait to receive a new date. When he did, the email read June 11, two days before he was due to graduate from Sullivan.

ALEJANDRO

•

Growing up in Guatemala City, Alejandro knew the landscape as a patchwork of gang territories. Though MS-13 was first established in Los Angeles by El Salvadorian refugees fleeing the civil war, it began to take hold of Central America in the 1990s when the U.S. government deported hundreds of members back to their home countries. By the time Alejandro was a boy, MS-13 had more than fifty thousand members among its ranks. They extorted money from business owners. They recruited young drug runners through threats of violence. Killers were celebrated as heroes, and dead gang members treated as martyrs. Remaining invisible was a fight for survival in city taken prisoner by violence.

For Alejandro, gunshots were part of the mix of neighborhood sounds. When kids went missing, he figured they had been killed. Some, however, were abducted and initiated into the gang and taught how to handle guns. MS-13 members were known to raid homes and canvas the neighborhood in black SUVs and trucks with tinted windows and no license plates. In a city plagued by violence, joining a gang could feel more like an inevitability than a choice. As much as possible, Alejandro stayed in his family home. Each venture out brought the threat of violence or an encounter with its aftermath. Many of these incidents still haunt him.

One afternoon, as Alejandro walked home from school, he watched as gang members in an SUV with tinted windows pulled up to a group of young men gathered at the corner and sprayed them with bullets. Alejandro saw body after body fall to the ground. He counted ten dead in the seconds before he sprinted away. Another time, he witnessed his neighbor, a widow who bravely pledged to testify in court against the MS-13 members who'd killed her son, get gunned down from a passing car as she mowed her front lawn.

Alejandro's stepfather, Edmundo, warned the boy against the gang life. Edmundo had been a member of the Eighteenth Street Gang, a longtime revival of MS-13, before he bought himself out. Years later, he was still haunted by his past. Edmundo drank—a lot. And when he did, Alejandro grew worried. Edmundo had a habit of stripping off his shirt and revealing the mosaic of Eighteenth Street insignias inked across his chest. It was a dangerous and deliberate move, one that Alejandro feared would lead to Edmundo's death. Eventually it did.

Alejandro was sleeping deeply when his younger brother came running into the room.

"My dad, my dad," his younger brother cried looking down at Alejandro, who still lay in bed. "Look what happened to my dad."

Alejandro pulled a shirt over his head and ran to the front of the house, where he found his mother. She was speaking with the police.

"Go back to your room," Luana instructed him. "Your dad . . . Your dad . . ."

Alejandro looked past his mother and saw his stepfather, shirtless, lying face down in the middle of the street. He had been shot twelve times in the chest.

In the years that followed, Alejandro watched as many of his friends enlisted in MS-13. He'd first notice them wearing nicer shoes and a blue and white rosary, a symbol of the gang. As new recruits, they were tasked with selling drugs and staking claim on corners in the city's escalating turf wars. But Alejandro, thinking of Edmundo, refused to join. His closest friend Jose, who was seven years his senior, resisted, too, which did not go unnoticed.

The first time members of MS-13 approached Jose, he and his friends were preparing for a water balloon fight. It was a hot, sticky afternoon. As the boys filled their balloons from a hose, a group of young men approached Jose. They handed the boy a letter.

"Read it out loud," one of the young men demanded. Jose, ever sure-footed and calm, looked over the letter quietly. When he finished he looked up.

"We're not going to do this," Jose responded. "We're not going to join."

"Then you're going to die," one of the young men said.

"We're good people," Jose continued. "We don't have issues with anyone. Let us be."

After that, Alejandro began to notice MS-13 members everywhere. They moved with a feral swagger. They drank beer in the alleys. They tucked knives into their shoes. They came and went as they pleased, untouchable. One afternoon, a group of young men approached Alejandro at school. They asked if he wanted to be friends. But friendship, Alejandro knew, came with a high price. After he refused one too many times, the same boys came looking for him with knives in hand. One managed to stab Alejandro in the arm and chest before Alejandro broke free and sprinted home. He still has scars where the metal broke his skin. But despite growing alarms, Alejandro felt secure with Jose around. Jose would, he thought, keep him safe.

The air was dusty in January 2013, the middle of the dry season in Guatemala City. Alejandro and Jose had just bought drinks from their preferred neighborhood convenience store. Alejandro usually bought bread—the woman who owned the store was the best baker in the neighborhood—but he refrained that day because he needed to save the money to buy water for showers and washing dishes at home. The boys took their sodas to the sidewalk curb. They sat at the edge and stretched their legs. Jose, who didn't have his phone, wanted to play a FIFA game. He told Alejandro to run home and borrow his mother's phone so the two could play. Alejandro obliged. The roundtrip took Alejandro, who prided himself on his speed, only a few minutes. On his way back, as he turned the corner and Jose came into view, Alejandro saw a black car pull up in front of his friend. He then heard several sharp cracks ring out. When the car pulled away, Jose's body lay flat on the sidewalk. A small pool of blood began to spread beneath his head. Jose was dead.

After Jose died, the only options that remained for Alejandro in Guatemala City were bad. Jose's brother framed it in simple terms: "If you stay with me, we're not gonna let no bitch kill us. We gonna be ready. They try to kill us, we kill them."

Alejandro had never picked up a gun and he didn't intend to.

So when Alejandro's uncle rode up outside Luana's house on a motorcycle less than a month after Jose was killed, Alejandro was already dressed in his Air Jordan sweatshirt and new sneakers. He was ready to leave. Luana handed Alejandro's uncle $4,000 in cash, the price of hiring a coyote to bring her son across Mexico and into the United States. She gave Alejandro a small card with an image of Jesus Christ and told him to pray every night. Alejandro's uncle hurried him along. They had to reach the Mexican border by the following day. Pulling himself up and over the motorcycle seat, Alejandro settled in behind his uncle and left Guatemala City for good.

The year Alejandro left Guatemala was the same year sixty-eight thousand unaccompanied minors fled to the U.S. border, many of whom sought to escape similar horror and pain in their home countries. By the time Alejandro started north, the number of undocumented children—mostly teens—apprehended at the border had doubled since the year prior.

Alejandro and his uncle road his motorcycle to the Mexico-Guatemala border where they crossed the Suchiate River into the state of Chiapas. From there, they met another four migrants hoping to reach the United States and a coyote, whose job it was to deliver the group to their destination. Alejandro spent eighteen days traveling the thousand miles from the southern tip of Mexico to the Rio Grande at the northern edge of the country. Sometimes the group would walk for ten hours before taking breaks. They slept in shifts, with at least one person always keeping guard.

Alejandro would eat once each day, street food such as tacos, tamales. The last two days were spent crossing the Chihuahuan Desert, a graveyard of migrant corpses. While Alejandro basked in the freedom of the desert expanse—he liked to sprint from the front of the group to the back—the terrain proved challenging for his uncle. He began to lag behind the group. When the coyote warned Alejandro that the group might have to leave his uncle behind, Alejandro refused.

"We came together, we stay together," Alejandro told the coyote. "If he stops, I stop, too. I'm not going to leave him in the desert."

When the coyote brought the group to a cabin at the edge of the Rio Grande, he told Alejandro and the others to wait for smugglers who would bring them across the river and into Texas. Alejandro waited in the cabin for three days. The river was one of the busiest and most dangerous crossings along the Mexico and U.S. border. The riverbed is uneven and the currents unpredictable. Taking one wrong step in the river could mean getting swept away. Some try to cross on inflatable pools. Others wade into the water wearing life jackets over their clothes. When the smugglers arrived, they told Alejandro he would hold on to a car tire and float to the Texas border.

The current was fast the day Alejandro crossed. And while the water looked shallow in some areas, other parts dipped without warning to a depth of eight feet. Debris floated at the surface, and the banks were littered with inflatable tubes and Styrofoam noodles. The coyote put him on a tire with a young girl, someone

Alejandro had never met, and the two clung to each other as the tire splashed in the current's wake.

Once on U.S. soil, Alejandro was apprehended by U.S. Customs and Border Protection agents and separated from his uncle. He was taken to a border station, a chaotic place filled with hundreds of young people who had recently crossed the border and were seeking asylum. The facility was one of dozens across the Southwest, where immigrant youth were kept while they waited to be given a court hearing and to be released to either family members or other individuals they knew. Alejandro spent six weeks inside the facility. The food was bad and the rooms dirty, but he was allowed to shower and play video games. That was enough to distract the thirteen-year-old.

Alejandro was flown to Chicago where he was released to the custody of his father, Sergio, who he hadn't seen in nearly a decade. He had almost no memory of Sergio. When Alejandro spoke to his father before leaving Guatemala, Sergio promised he would buy his son whatever he wanted. But new shoes couldn't solve what felt like an insurmountable problem. Sergio felt like a total stranger to Alejandro. The only image Alejandro had of him was from pictures at his grandmother's house. But when he walked out into the airport corridor, Alejandro recognized Sergio right away. He knew his eyes. Sergio was holding a hand-drawn sign that read "Welcome" and his cheeks were wet with tears.

The first night in his father's apartment was one of Alejandro's loneliest. He and Sergio spent much of that night in silence. They watched Disney's *Cars*. Alejandro, who knew almost no English then, required Spanish subtitles.

One evening, when Alejandro particularly missed his home, he made one of his mother's recipes, which included white onion and garlic. He hoped it would connect the two men to their lost home. Sergio didn't like to talk about his previous life in Guatemala. But when Sergio took a bite, he spit out the food.

"Why did you do that?" Alejandro asked, distraught by his father's reaction.

"I don't eat onions," Sergio responded. "But you didn't know."

The episode left Alejandro feeling excruciatingly alone. He had spent so much of his childhood longing for his father. He had fantasized about what it would mean to see him again. But now that Alejandro lay on his futon bed in an unfamiliar apartment in a country where he didn't speak the language nor had any promise of permanence, he longed for Guatemala. And no matter how much time passed, that was an ache that he never could quite shake.

6

JANUARY

Sarah Quintenz

By the time school starts back up after winter break, the holiday cheer that animated the halls has given way to bitter, if not morose, winter doldrums. The school floors, now a bright white thanks to a $120,000 renovation over the break, are wet from melted snow and ice drips from students' boots. Winter sports—basketball, volleyball, wrestling—will begin in just a few weeks, their seasons marked by a pep rally where students fill the auditorium with blue and yellow balloons and streamers. The day is a bright spot among the dregs of winter. Hoping to join the wrestling team and take the stage at the rally, a group of Rohingya boys have started a weight-lifting club. They visit the second-floor weight room every day after school and observe how their classmates work their thighs, chests, and biceps, each muscle group demanding a different set of machines. The boys study every motion as they watch their seasoned classmates, but by February, several will have dropped out, preferring to spend time playing FIFA or billiards on their phones.

———————

When Sarah walks out of three hours of meetings, the sun has already begun to set. As she makes her way toward her office she has one thing on her mind: Samir, a Syrian senior, cannot be made to repeat his final year. Forcing him to stay another year would be devastating to him. He has five days to make up his missing work from the fall. If he doesn't, his whole school year will be lost and he will likely never get an American high school degree.

Samir arrived at Sullivan in 2016 with a wave of Syrian students, all of them fleeing the Syrian civil war that has made refugees of almost six million people. Samir was already fully bearded when he arrived at Sullivan and looked like a teacher. Like many older Syrian students, Samir had completed high school in Syria but he did not have time to gather his documents when he fled the country.

Even though he probably never should have had to enroll in a U.S. high school, Samir has registered at Sullivan on multiple occasions since he rarely sticks with school for more than a few months at a time. But Sarah advocates for him each time he comes back. Lately, she has run out of negotiating room. His latest chance, which began in September, would likely be his last. When Samir showed up to re-enroll at Sullivan at the beginning of the year, Sarah informed him he'd be "on the shortest leash ever." No mistakes. No missing work. No fights. By January, Samir's record was marked mainly by the exact missteps Sarah warned him against.

Sarah first heard reports of a fight from other students.

Rumor was the brawl started when Samir confronted a freshman American-born boy who he overheard cursing at a female classmate. Samir, who is broad chested with a square jaw, and who towered over the freshman, confronted the name-caller. Within seconds, Samir took a punch to the face. Shortly after that, a small army of boys descended on Samir.

The fight was just one of several between Syrian boys and their Black American classmates, which usually arose from miscommunication and clashing egos. Often when such tensions boiled over, Danny Rizk was asked to mitigate in both Arabic and English. On one such occasion, an older Syrian sophomore was eating popcorn and joking around in Arabic in his Spanish class, a period that included both ELL and native English speakers. When the Syrian boy made eye contact with a Black American classmate, the American took the glance as a threat.

"Shut the fuck up," he told his Syrian classmate.

"Suck my dick," the Syrian boy responded.

"I'll fucking kill you."

News of the brewing tension soon made its way to Danny. But by the time Danny found the Syrian student, the sophomore had already left school and returned with a friend. One had a chain wrapped around his hand and the other carried a lead pipe, which he'd removed from a vacuum cleaner. The boy and his friend were used to fending for themselves while living in exile. Danny, who is sinewy but slight, pulled Antoine Livingston and the security staff into the mix. Both students were suspended for two weeks, and the school staff put a long-term safety plan in place when they returned.

Most misunderstandings did not escalate to violence. Instead, Danny usually played interlocutor for smaller clashes like two boys bumping each other or volleying foul insults. When issues of race and racism arose, like when Syrian boys asked Danny misguided questions such as why their Black classmates were poor and violent, Danny did not reprimand their ignorance. Instead, he offered them a truncated lesson in American history. "Okay so," he'd say, "when this country was started four hundred years ago, they brought people from Africa in chains. They would beat them and make them work for free. After two hundred years, they said the slaves were free, but they weren't really. This country has always been unfair to Black people."

Race was not the only issue Sarah and her staff tackled in the ELL "womb." They also discussed gender dynamics, a topic that elicited a variety of responses. Sarah, for one, wrote *A woman needs a man like a fish needs a bicycle* on the office whiteboard when a senior boy insisted that women depended on men. Ihina, who was in the room, offered her classmate another perspective. "Y'all be thirsty for girls with big boobs and big heels," she told him. "We don't need you; you need *us*. We strong. We don't need no men at all."

The most common discussions, however, focused on matters of the heart.

Among those lovesick students who regularly came to the "womb" was Nassim, a Syrian freshman. On one such occasion, Nassim, who was tall and clumsy as though midway through a growth spurt, came barreling into the ELL office, letting out a series of anguished groans as he threw himself against the file cabinet and pressed his forehead against the metal drawers, leaning his entire weight against it.

"This is really an emergency," he explained to Sarah as he moved to the doorframe, bouncing his agitated body from one side to the other. "It's so bad. It's this girl in my class. She says she like me."

Sarah cued up the R & B song "Sukiyaki" by 4 P.M. on her computer. She mouthed along to the crooner confessional, holding the words "you" and "blue" just a beat longer than the rest.

"Well, I write an email asking her if she likes any boys in the class," Nassim continued. "She wrote back and said she liked one boy in the class. So I said, you mean me?"

"What'd you do then?" Sarah prodded.

"I go out of the class. I came here. I don't know what to do."

"Honey, this is just your first experience," said Sarah, "That nervous feeling you have in the bottom of your stomach is the best and worst feeling. Get used to it. It's a good thing."

"I'm not excited. My body is all nervous. It feels bad, man."

"It's *haram*?" Sarah asked trying to understand what he means.

"Yeah, what if my brothers find out. They might hit me

because they don't want me with a girl. Not a Mexican girl. And they will start making stuff up and tell my parents."

"If your brothers do that, you tell me," said Sarah. "I will call your house. Hell, I will go to your house. I will talk to your family."

By the following Monday, Nassim's flirtation had turned to a relationship. Five days later, the romance had run its course.

But when Samir told Sarah about the cafeteria fight, he wasn't seeking wisdom. The senior spun it his own way: "One hero and seventeen hundred babies," he told her. In Samir's version, he was the hero standing up for women. The telling made Sarah laugh. Samir always made Sarah laugh. When Samir would regale Sarah, he'd often begin with the same opening line: "I have a good story. Enjoy." Samir would amuse Sarah with reports of his father's absentee parenting. "He thinks it's just like watching a movie," he'd say. "He watch and do nothing." If his father's behavior sounded careless, Samir never narrated it that way. He'd tell her about his brief affair with a Ukrainian woman. At first, he recounted their weekend-long dates at a Wisconsin golf club where the two would spend the entire day poolside surrounded by potted palm trees. When the girl broke up with Samir, he cried to Sarah. The breakup, he said, had been a stab in the heart. Samir also shared stories about long nights at his favorite hookah bar, Cairo Nights, and the time a police officer pulled him over for reckless driving. He was an endless source of new stories.

The fight, however, came with more serious consequences. Together, Sarah and Samir decided he should transfer to Harry S. Truman Middle College, an institution that gives students like Samir the flexibility to earn their degree while still working full-time. But before leaving for good, Samir got one final chance. He could come to Sullivan and spend time in the library to catch up on homework, but he could not attend the classes. If he completed the assignments, he could likely graduate in June. It wasn't an impossible proposal. Samir, after all, had been through high school already. He just needed to discipline himself to do the work. So far, he had not. He sat in the library falling behind every day.

Refugee students can end up leaving Sullivan for any number of reasons. Oftentimes, families move. Sometimes students collapse under the pressure to both attend school and work to support their families. Other students marry and simply disappear. Sarah will give students as many chances as she can to return to school. If Sarah could keep Samir at Sullivan, she would. But now, no matter what, his last semester before graduation will be at another institution, on someone else's watch.

Back in her office, Sarah sits down next to Samir who's been waiting for her. He's only halfway through his day but Samir is cranky. He spent the morning on reading questions related to Paul Fleischman's young adult novel *Seedfolks*, a story about how immigrant groups in Cleveland come together around a community garden. Samir's had enough. He wants to go home to rest before he starts his evening shift at work.

As he complains, students begin to pour into the office. Among them is Ihina who throws herself down into a seat. She puts a container of instant ramen in the microwave and swivels toward Samir.

"Damn, it smells like someone got their period in here," she says. "It smells like *shit*."

Sarah, who thoroughly enjoys Ihina, laughs. Samir looks on in astonishment. He may like to entertain, but he can't compete with Ihina.

"I can't eat my noodles in here," Ihina continues, now gripping her Maruchan cup. "I'm out."

The Nepalese senior disappears as quickly as she arrived. She'll be back in a couple hours to do her makeup—a multi-step process that requires the office mirror—before heading to Devon Avenue, where she works the phones at an Indian restaurant. Sarah looks forward to it.

Looking at Samir, Sarah tells him that he has to work through his American history homework first. She starts with the basics.

"Who wrote the Constitution?" she asks him, looking over a worksheet provided by Samir's history teacher.

He looks at her blankly. She tries another. "Who is John Adams? What about George Washington?"

Samir shrugs. "Ma, why do you make me learn this?" he protests.

"Come on, man," Sarah replies. "You have to try."

"I don't have to study this thing, it's not my business."

"If you want to become an American citizen you do."

"I just want to graduate. I don't care from where," Samir says. "Here, next door, heaven, the moon. I just want to finish. I am too old."

"Yeah," says Sarah, "this is why you broke my heart."

"But I love you, Ma," he says, genuinely.

"I love you, too."

The following week, Annmarie Handley marches Nassim into the ELL office. Today's issue has nothing to do with young love. Standing inside the door, Nassim wears his Junior Reserve Officers' Training Corps uniform, which includes a camel-colored army shirt paired with navy slacks. The uniform also includes a plastic-molded rifle, which Nassim slings over his shoulder, but he left the prop in Annmarie's classroom. Annmarie explains that Nassim has been throwing up gang gestures in her classroom and in the hallways. She says she's seen it herself and other students have reported it to her as well. She asks Sarah to explain to Nassim what the gestures signify and the dangers he might face flashing them in the wrong crowd. Teachers often delegate these kinds of tasks to Sarah, perhaps because she is "the cool teacher" the students trust with the details of their lives.

Sarah looks at Nassim. She often sees him zipping from one end of the school to the other, his head and shoulders leaning slightly forward and a camera hanging from his neck. He is one of the yearbook photographers and has a talent with portraits in natural light. His images capture students bent over classroom chemistry experiments and playing guitar in a nook of the first floor. Sarah is certain Nassim is ignorant of what he's doing when flashing coded gestures. She asks him to show her the symbols he's been making. He giggles and raises his left hand.

"Are you kidding me?" she says to Nassim. "What do you think you're doing? This isn't a joke." Sarah pauses with an idea. She makes her way toward the door. "Follow me."

Sarah marches the boy down the first-floor hallway and to the school cafeteria. Pushing her way through the swinging wood door, she tells Nassim to wait against the wall by the security guards who are stationed there. She walks into the cafeteria, a wide room that's alive with noise. She circles the space, eventually landing at a table where a group of teenagers eat their lunch. She returns to Nassim with two boys from the table.

"Nassim, show these guys what you showed me earlier."

The boy shakes his head sheepishly. He's embarrassed to

repeat the gesture. She encourages him again. Nassim relents and lifts his hand, showing what looks like a shadow puppet of a bull. The boys shake their heads, demonstrably signaling how wrong Nassim is to experiment with such fire.

"Okay," one boy begins gently, "you are throwing up signs and it's not your sign. You're in Rogers Park and you are going to get into it with everybody if you don't stop."

"Will you please explain to him why he cannot do this?" Sarah pushes. "We're not making fun of him. We're not bullying him. We're just going to explain why he cannot do that anymore because he doesn't understand."

The second boy joins in. "I mean, yeah, you'll get beat up. Killed. There will be all kinds of problems for you. That's not your gang sign and when you do that you could end up in the hospital or worse. You could lose your parents. I've lost a lot of people: parents, cousins, friends, siblings. I'm trying to turn my life around so I don't lose any more."

"This is the wrong neighborhood for that," the first adds on. "This is life or death."

"It's not funny," adds Sarah looking at Nassim. "This is not a joke. Just listen to what these guys said."

"We're all family here," one boy adds. "We got your back in here. If y'all have problems, come to me. I got y'all. We're cool in here, but outside if you do that shit? Bye."

"Now shake hands because we're friends," Sarah instructs. The three follow Sarah's direction. She thanks the boys and tells them they can return to their lunch table. Before she delivers Nassim back to class she turns to him.

"I don't want to see you doing those hand signs again, okay? It's not a joke." Nassim nods and speeds inside the classroom. Sarah pivots toward the library and yells, "Love you!"

7

FEBRUARY

Mariah

Mariah walks into class looking fierce. She marches to her seat, but cannot settle down. She fidgets and chews at her already short fingernails. She plants her hands firmly and flatly on her thighs, trying to keep them still. It does not work. Her hands raise to push her thick, shiny black hair from one side of her head to the other, almost as if she were posing for a camera. A boy across the room tries to catch her eye. He tilts his head. A comb jutting from his hair nearly falls out. She sends him a withering stare, eyebrow arched, a playful grin on her face. Mariah knows what she wants: the boy's phone.

Mariah doesn't have a phone of her own, but manages a strong social media diet with small doses of screen time on other students' devices. She's starved for one now. She's missed several classes—and time on the others' phones—due to the ACCESS test, the onerous yearly ritual she, and nearly every other student in the state who is not a native English speaker, must take. The test's cumbersome full name—Assessing Comprehension and Communication in English State-to-State for English Language Learners—was almost certainly coined with the acronym in mind, but its length does at least reflect the duration of the exam, which lasts several hours and is administered every winter in the public schools. Mariah loathes the ACCESS test. After five years in the United States, she's fluent in spoken English and she's recently started reading young adult English-language books on her own, too. Her current favorite is *The Hate U Give*, about a teenage girl struggling to balance her life growing up in a mostly Black neighborhood while attending a school where the other students are mostly affluent and white. Mariah relates to the heroine's efforts to navigate two contrasting worlds.

The boy hands over his phone. Mariah logs into Snapchat. The app has been taken over by Valentine's Day buzz. The screen fills with pictures of roses, of stuffed bears holding boxes of chocolates and other sweet things in pink and white. And, of course, there's Cupid. Newer refugee students, most of whom Mariah doesn't talk to, but whose posts she sees, are particularly cupid crazed. They fill their Snapchat stories with lovesick messages such as *If you got the moon, don't lose the stars. Never ignore a person who loves you because one day you might wake up and realize you lose the moon while counting the stars.*

Holding up the camera, Mariah tilts her chin upward and chooses one Snapchat filter that lays an assortment of pulsing hearts above her head. She may not have a phone, but Mariah still knows her best angles.

"Alright," says Jocelyn Vale, Mariah's American history

teacher. "I want everyone thinking about their ideas on how to make the school better. You are going to create a thoughtful bill that will improve the productivity or environment of the classroom or school."

The bill, she tells the room, needs to be something realistic. Not, for example, to turn every lesson into a *SpongeBob SquarePants* viewing. Mariah stares stonily at her teacher. Why would she want to watch a children's cartoon? Jocelyn came to Sullivan this year as part of the class of new teachers whose positions are partially funded by the additional dollars that CPS gave to Sullivan to bolster the school's ELL program. She hopes the activity in today's lesson plan will motivate students to engage with school life and help them come to understand how passing bills in the U.S. legislature works.

"If you want something to change, you have to do something about it," Jocelyn continues. "So take this as your opportunity to practice that. And yes, every single one of you can have influence on our government, whether you're eighteen or not. Whether you're a citizen or not, you still live here."

Mariah takes this in. There's a lot about Sullivan she'd like to change.

"But that doesn't mean it's going to work," one student responds.

"You're right. But what's the point of not trying? If you don't try, there's a one hundred percent chance it won't work."

The teacher continues. She describes her grading schematic. Everyone in the class will have to propose a bill and vote on their classmates' bills. Jocelyn starts tossing out ideas on how to improve the school. What about more extracurriculars? she asks. A longer passing period? More snacks? Mariah raises her hand.

"What about getting rid of school uniforms?" she asks.

"Sure, that's good," Jocelyn responds. "But you'll need the votes."

Mariah has a stake in her proposal. School dress has made her unhappy since she entered high school. First, prior to Sullivan, at her previous high school, Mariah was one of only a few Muslim students. When she began her freshman year in 2016, she felt as if the entire school were talking about her headscarf. Her classmates peppered Mariah with questions about Islam. Some whispered "ISIS" when she passed them in the hallways. Mariah, at a loss then, watched how her older sister Farha negotiated the halls. She had always looked up to Farha, and whatever Farha did, Mariah followed suit. Farha, Mariah discovered, took off her hijab when she arrived at school. When Mariah still had her own phone, she saw her sister's selfies on social media, Farha's hair cascading down her back. Farha smoked cigarettes behind the school and drove around with boys in their cars. After their parents went to bed, her sister spent hours talking on the phone. Sometimes Mariah stayed up to listen. A month into her freshman year, Mariah decided to remove her hijab, too. She and Farha would arrive at school an hour early and head directly to the girls' bathroom.

There, Mariah would stuff her headscarf in her backpack and, when her classmates asked her where she was from, Mariah, who spoke with a Boricua flare ever since she began learning English from her Puerto Rican middle school classmates, told them she was from Puerto Rico. It seemed few remembered her headscarf.

By the time Mariah enrolled at Sullivan, Farha had left Chicago. She moved out after the girls' mother challenged them over a Snapchat story she heard about. It showed Farha and Mariah posed in tight tops without their hijabs, and in front of the neighborhood McDonald's. Farha dropped out of high school and in quick order was engaged to a cousin in Atlanta. The news crushed Mariah. She thought Farha was far too young to marry. She spent weeks cursing her sister, berating her for choosing marriage so young. Farha soon shut Mariah out. "It's not your business," she'd say. "I'm making my own choices."

Mariah heard from another cousin, a young woman who completed two years at Sullivan before dropping out to get married and pregnant. The cousin said that Sullivan was a welcoming place for Muslims, so Mariah decided she'd try the hijab again. She figured it would cheer up her mother, too. Mariah's battles with her mother over the hijab had nearly ripped her family apart. She wanted to repair the damage.

Her first lunch period at Sullivan was on the late side. At that hour in the fall, light poured sideways into the cafeteria in the geometric shapes of the windows. Mariah surveyed the cafeteria for signs of a crowd she might fit into. It appeared to her that every table hosted a different group. One corner of the room was occupied with a few boys—Rohingya, Iraqi, and African, throwing around a soccer ball across the cafeteria's blue linoleum floor. In another, a group of American kids blasted the latest hit from the Brooklyn-based rapper 6ix9ine. Mariah knew the song. She heard it often. Loud, reflexive shouts mixed with the heavy hip-hop beats rose from the center of the room where a group of girls watched videos on their cell phones. Most of them wore less conservative gambar and pashmina hijab styles, but they spoke a language that Mariah could not parse.

Still sussing out where she belonged, Mariah made her way to a table of Arabic-speaking girls in layered hijabs paired with trench coats tied over their school uniforms. Mariah could tell from their Levantine Arabic that most of the girls hailed from Syria. When she sat down, she greeted the girls in Arabic. A few smiled politely, while others ignored her. Mariah soon learned that the girls saw their clique as a cut above their Sullivan community. They complained that they could not attend gym class because it was *haram*. Discussing human anatomy in biology is *haram*. Teachers who wore sleeveless tops in class? Very *haram*. Whatever cordiality they mustered toward Mariah that first day soon soured. A few days in, Mariah spied the girls mocking her turban-style hijab. They wrote to one another over text. *Why would she wear a scarf at all? What kind of Muslim is she, anyway?* After that, Mariah left her hijab at home. If her former school felt unwelcoming to Muslims, these Muslim mean girls were no better.

Mariah soon fell back into her bad habits. She skipped class. She rarely wore her uniform. When Sullivan security guards reprimanded her, she rolled her eyes ostentatiously. By November, Mariah was notorious among Sullivan staff. Whenever staff would address Mariah, her answers were pointed and sardonic.

Just two months into the new year, Matt Fasana heard Mariah had been causing trouble. He called a meeting with the girl and her mother.

As Mariah and her mother, Fatmeh, stood outside Matt's door, the sophomore was filled with dread. Meetings with school staff, she knows, can sometimes prove dangerous.

A little over a year ago, the worst day of Mariah's life started at the mirror. It was a chilly morning in early January, early enough in the year that Christmas lights still hung from shop windows. Mariah stood in the bathroom, door closed, examining the scratch and bruise around her eye. Fatmeh, in what she said was an accident, had hit Mariah in the face in an attempt to stop a fight between Mariah and one of her brothers. When Mariah arrived at school, she was immediately peppered with questions about her bruises. The first few times she was asked, Mariah explained she'd gotten in a fight with a friend. But when one of her teachers asked, Mariah broke down and revealed the truth. She explained that she and her brother had been fighting when her mom hit her in the face. Mariah's teacher called a social worker to the room and Mariah repeated the story. When she did, the social worker explained that they planned to call the Department of Children and Family Services and an investigator would likely visit her parents to inquire about her home life. The investigator's job, he said, was to determine if Mariah was living in a safe environment. The news sunk Mariah. Reporting the incident had been a mistake. What if an investigation broke their family apart? What if they tried to deport her parents back to Iraq? What if they deported her? There were no good outcomes to this news. *Fuck it*, Mariah thought to herself.

Later that day, when the sun had nearly set, Fatmeh discovered Mariah looking dazed on the couch.

"Mariah, you look tired," Fatmeh said in Arabic, leaning over her daughter.

"I took a pill from the counter by mistake," Mariah explained. "Ibuprofen. I had stomach pain."

Fatmeh told her daughter to drink some water. Mariah complied, but her pain did not subside. A few minutes later, Fatmeh, increasingly concerned, asked Mariah again. "What did you take? How many pills did you take?"

"Three," Mariah said, offering a new answer to the question.

"Be honest, Mariah," Fatmeh urged. "How many did you take? Do you want me to take you to the hospital?"

"No."

Fatmeh pushed again. Mariah was fading quickly.

"What did you take, Mariah?" Fatmeh now asked, panicked. Before Mariah could answer, she keeled over and spewed green vomit on the living room rug.

"How many pills did you take," Fatmeh begged. "Just tell me, Mariah."

"Eight pills . . . a handful . . . I don't know."

"Why? Because of the scratch on your face? Why would you do this?"

"You don't know what I did," Mariah said.

"Whatever you did, it's not worth losing your life over," Fatmeh said, reaching for her daughter. "Just tell me what you took."

"I took Dad's pills. I feel like I'm dying, I can't breathe. I'm dying."

By now, several of Fatmeh's children had gathered around Mariah. Alaa, Mariah's eldest brother, jumped to action. He took Mariah up in his arms and ran her down the flight of stairs to his car. Fatmeh followed.

Mariah could barely hold herself up in the back seat of the car.

"Open the windows," she begged. "I can't breathe."

"Drive faster," Fatmeh screamed at Alaa, who was navigating to the hospital. "Your sister is dying."

"Do you want us to die in a car accident?" Alaa shouted back. "I'm going as fast as I can."

The ER nurses pumped Mariah's stomach when she arrived at the hospital. She remained delirious for two days, including when the DCFS social worker came to interview her. She told them her father had died in a car accident. She said a nurse had hit her and claimed she could hear the television speaking. Fatmeh sat by the hospital bed day and night. She was also interviewed through a translator. She cried and swore there had been some misunderstanding. Hitting Mariah had been an accident, she said. The room had been dark and when Fatmeh tried to pull Mariah and her brother apart, she had elbowed Mariah in the eye. Once lucid, Mariah seconded her mother's version of events. It had all been a mistake, Mariah said. After several more interviews and a home visit, the DCFS investigator closed the case.

Mariah spent almost a week in an austere single room on the second floor of the psychiatric ward at Lurie Children's Hospital. Inside her room, Mariah wasn't allowed to keep food, electronics, or even wear a bra. She barely spoke in her group therapy sessions for the first two days. When the counselor would call on Mariah, she always responded the same way.

"I don't need to be here," she repeated.

"There's nothing you want to talk about?" the counselor asked.

"No. Like I said, I don't need to be here. Everything is misunderstood."

Mariah did, however, listen as other patients told their stories. She was particularly drawn toward one boy who explained he had no one waiting for him outside the hospital walls. Mariah, whose own loneliness could cripple her at times, understood the feeling. But her family came to the hospital every day. They brought her food. They filled her in on family gossip. They asked about her health. No one ever came to visit the boy.

After a couple days in group therapy, Mariah realized that she would never get released if she didn't start talking. So she opened up. Mariah explained that she fought her parents on everything in America. She wanted to live an American life, but her parents held on to traditional, conservative Iraqi values. The gulf between generations sometimes felt insurmountable. Mariah often pondered why her parents came to America if they were going to just hold on to those ideas, a contradiction she could not understand.

When Mariah was released from the hospital, her father came to pick her up. She told him she had a matter she wanted to discuss.

"Dad," Mariah said in Arabic, "I'm not going to wear the hijab any more. I'm done."

"Okay, Mariah," he replied. "Whatever you want. I just want you out of here."

As they drove through the Chicago streets, Mariah watched

the city pass by through the window. Christmas lights were still up. She'd only been gone for a week, but it felt like a lifetime had passed.

When Matt waved Mariah and Fatmeh into his office, Mariah quietly took a seat in the corner. She pressed her hands against her thighs, though everything about the meeting made Mariah want to flail or shout or leave. Instead, she steeled herself to her mother's coming fury. But Matt was kind. His even demeanor emanated authority, concern, and optimism all at once. He thanked Fatmeh for coming. He told her that he thought Mariah was nice, but obstinate. Fatmeh nodded in agreement. Mariah had heard her scream *aneeda*, the Arabic word for willful, at her hundreds of times.

"We're a proud community," Matt continued. "We really want to push that we're family. That we're together. We also want to just check in and see how you're doing. How are you liking Sullivan?"

"Good," Mariah replied. "Like last year, I had a lot of drama at school. And I decided I wanted to be a better person and I wanted a new school with a fresh start. When I came to Sullivan, I started doing better. And I've been better."

Matt asked her about her previous problems.

"Like drama," Mariah responded, careful not to reveal too many details. "It was stupid stuff. Telling your business to other people."

Then Fatmeh spoke. "I see she is better here," she said, looking at her daughter. "She feel good. She get along with people. At her old school, there is nobody there like her. So she feel bad there. And after her sister married, she feel more bad. I know, she do something wrong. I always fight with her about clothes."

"We have that in common," laughed Matt.

"Okay," Fatmeh answered, shifting in her chair. "Give her a chance. She can be better."

Another Tuesday Afternoon

February afternoons in Chicago Public Schools can be bleak. Looking outside the classroom windows in October or April may inspire daydreams about walks under the colored leaves or budding flowers. But daydreaming about gray, icy February in the city promises far fewer delights. The sounds of car owners scraping their windshields or skidding at the stop signs can be heard in the classrooms. Outside, sooty snow, stained with dog waste, ensures a cold and depressing walk home. Inside Sullivan, the bright lights of the classrooms oddly intensify the dark of the day, and the building is a mix of stifling, overheated (and drafty, under-heated) halls and rooms. Students come to school packing all sorts of tinctures, pastes, and bottles of misted remedies to ward off all the infections they generically call "flu." It is in February when students who fled warmer climates long most intensely and vocally for the heat they left.

For Sarah and the young ELL teachers at Sullivan, a break from the cold is still six to ten weeks away. The energy of the weekly Tuesday afternoon ELL department meeting begins low, and Sarah knows it will sink lower still as the sun sets. But Sarah works to conjure enthusiasm among the bunch: "It's pretty cool that we get paid overtime to have these meetings," she says, placing her laptop computer at the end of the table. "We're happy to be here. We're excited to get organized. Yay." Chips, cookies, coffee, staples of teacher meetings, also fuel the group past the late-day lull.

The meeting agenda covers far more than the usual organizational puzzles. Sarah needs enthusiasm and energy from the room to conquer the bigger challenge of Sullivan's ELL curriculum. This is the second swipe at evaluating the school's program since the year began. Among those resources that make Sullivan's ELL program unique are specialized tutoring, smaller classes, and a social worker dedicated to working with the school's ELL population. Sarah also maintains close partnerships with local resettlement agencies and neighborhood organizations that provide counseling, food, and after-school programs for refugee and immigrant teens. With the revamp also comes a grand new name, Sullivan's International Academy. For this meeting, Sarah has invited Ambareen Nasir, an educational consultant and lecturer at Loyola University—the university is among Sullivan's partners—who will lead the meeting. Her research focuses, in part, on preparing green

ELL teachers. Sarah brought her in to speak about methods that work in the classroom.

"Thank you for having me here," Ambareen says, looking out at the group and their full plates of snacks. "And welcome to today's session on "What do we stand for? What is our vision for the ELL program here? Today we're establishing a vision."

Ambareen asks someone to read the department's current vision statement. A teacher toward the end of the table volunteers.

"The International Academy offers a comprehensive program that will meet the academic, social, and emotional needs of students and their families," she recites from her open laptop. It's the kind of muffled, drone-ish delivery most teachers would interrupt were it a student speaking. "We work in partnership with refugee agencies, elementary schools, and community organizations to provide a seamless experience to transition into American culture." The recitation seems to speed the sun's descent outside.

Ambareen asks the same woman to read the mission statement. The woman complies.

"To provide a strong education for all of our students and help them to become participatory citizens in the democratic society," she says, "life-long learners, and productive working members of their local communities." Outside, the streetlamps begin to glow.

Ambareen asks the group to meditate on these statements and write a short reaction to them. Once they've finished she encourages everyone to read over the responses, which they put into a shared Google document.

"I don't want to call people out," says one of the newest teachers in the bunch, "I just read something interesting. 'We give them the tools to become productive Americans.' I didn't really like that. We never really use that descriptor. I'm wondering what tools do we provide?"

Sarah jumps in: "And what does it even mean to be an American?"

"And does that define character?" adds another.

"I like that we all have this idea that it is good to pay it forward," says Sarah. "That we're helping the students as newcomers, but then when they leave here, it's their job to help another newcomer along the way."

After quickly scanning the groups' responses, Ambareen jumps in to focus the conversation. She is politic and careful with her words as she knows it's late and that complaints from a tired room of teachers can spiral. "I'm seeing some shared goals," she says, "Transitioning into American culture. Mentorship. Strategy. What we want to do today is try and unpack what all of this means."

"Advocacy and having a voice is important," adds Sarah. "We have to teach them that in this country you vote for everything. Even when you're in the classroom, you vote."

"I think it should be two separate ideas because being a

citizen is not just about voting," responds another teacher at the table. "It's about having responsibility to your country, community, and family."

They continue back and forth. These are big ideas that sit at the heart of Sullivan's mission, and ones that feel particularly urgent in an era of increasing nativism. But they are not easily defined. Ambareen does not interrupt. The issues, she finds, should be hashed out by teachers. To push them with students, they have to feel they are the guides in the framing of the ideas.

Dirk Casto speaks up. "Can I just say something? We used to have more of a global view and now it's a very narrow view. It's like American citizenship. In the past, we've emphasized world citizens. These kids are not trapped here, and they need to learn how to be successful on a global scale."

Everyone around the table nods in assent. Ambareen suggests they add the thought to the mission statement.

"Again," she says, "Today we are developing the core ideas that will make Sullivan's ELL program different from the rest. These ideas should be your North Star."

Ambareen breaks up the room into groups. She tells them to work in the shared Google drive. In one group, the conversation quickly derails into an argument on whether classes should be taught as bilingual curriculums. And then into whether teachers should be native speakers of the students' languages. To do that, the school would need a staff of translators bigger than the U.N.'s to offer native proficiency to all the students. In another group, Dirk and Josh talk about the reality that students are often expected to work and take care of their families. Most stick to their own culture and language both inside and out of school.

"Have you heard about the hidden curriculum?" Dirk asks Josh. "It's what kids pick up outside of class. There's a strong hidden curriculum in Sullivan, it's what American culture they're picking up from other kids in the building. That's also something Sullivan offers." Because Sullivan has not only a critical mass of refugee and other immigrant children, but also an American-born student body, teenagers new to America can draw on the collective intelligence of both groups to help digest and acclimate to their new world.

Josh and Dirk continue to brainstorm ideas. Dirk squints at his laptop screen. "Who says that students should have a seamless transition into American culture?" he asks looking over another teacher's answer on the shared document. "Nothing about this process is seamless. If anything, it's a road full of speed bumps. America is a corporatocracy full of gringos. God, that sounds so dark, doesn't it?"

"Really, this whole exercise is about navigating what it means to be an immigrant in America," adds Josh.

"It's true, though," says Dirk. "At the end of the day, they'll be treated like people who have an accent." Josh starts to write the thought, but he erases it. That's a conversation for another day.

Chad Adams

Chad excels in a crisis. This week tested how many he could juggle at the same time. Just past midnight on Monday, February 20, Antoine Livingston texted Chad an image grabbed from Snapchat, a low-angle selfie of a Sullivan senior shirtless, smiling, and holding a gun in his left hand. The boy stared down at the camera, his smile lines visible on either side of a muted grin. Overlaid on the image, the boy had typed the words: *I'm shooting up Sullivan tomorrow :)*

Chad knew the kid; he was a goof. He could have just been mugging for the camera. Snapchat is like Hollywood for high schoolers and they playact on it. But he also knew that he couldn't take the threat lightly. The week before, on February 14, at Marjory Stoneman Douglas High School in Parkland, Florida, a student opened fire with a semi-automatic weapon, killing seventeen people. School shootings have been on the rise across the country since a gunman killed twenty first-graders and six adults at Sandy Hook Elementary School in 2012. Over the past five years, there have been at least 239 school shootings nationwide. Across them, 438 people have been shot, and 138 of them killed. In the days following the shooting at Parkland, the Chicago Police Department had been fielding dozens of shooting threats. Last Chad heard, the police department had flagged twenty-five threats that identified Chicago public high schools as targets.

The following morning, Chad drafted an email to send to all Sullivan parents. His skill at such notes had been drilled into him during his career in the system. In 2012, at his last school on Chicago's South Side, Harper High School, twenty-nine current or recent students were shot. Chad had developed a gift for finding the right words for notes to worried parents, but writing them never gets easy. He put the new communication on Sullivan digital letterhead, white paper with blue trim and the school insignia, an *S* with a tiger sitting on it. The school's motto, "Learning is alive through everything we do and everywhere we go," appears in the top righthand corner.

> Dear Parents and Guardians,
>
> We want to make you aware of a situation involving our school in recent days.
>
> Late last night, a student shared a social media posting that resembled a potential threat against the school. The Chicago Police Department and CPS Office of Safety and Security [were] immediately notified to investigate this threat. Upon completion of their assessment, the Chicago Police Department deemed the threat was not credible and there was no risk to student or staff.
>
> Your child's safety will always be our highest priority. If you have any questions, please do not hesitate to contact the school.

When the boy arrived at Sullivan on Tuesday morning, the police were waiting for him on the corner. He never did make it into the building. They arrested him on the spot. By the afternoon, Chad learned from the police that the gun in the photo was a fake that belonged to the boy's grandfather. A prank gone too far. In fact, he'd spent the morning dropping his brother off at a nearby elementary school. Chad transferred the boy to an alternative school and he asked the police not to charge him.

Before Chad arrived at Sullivan, the school operated strictly through punitive forms of punishment. Some years, the number of in-school suspensions totaled more than five hundred. One of Chad's first moves as principal was eliminating the camera-monitored suspension room and replacing it with a peace room. The room, which sits on the second floor and boasts a clear view of the city skyline, is where Chad and his staff now run peace circles, a restorative practice that encourages students to come together to repair harm through conversation.

Peace circles, however, did not replace Sullivan's full-time security staff or the two Chicago police officers in the building. Keeping students safe inside the Sullivan building is an ever-changing challenge, and one Chad believes requires a multipronged approach. The Chicago police, for one, still have not identified who shot Esengo. School shootings are on the rise, and there doesn't seem to be any effective way to predict them. Warm weather, too, will inevitably bring news of an uptick in violent crime across Chicago. Worse, yet, Chad worries the national temper may be shifting violently toward his immigrant, refugee, and especially Muslim students.

Threats fill Chad's thoughts when he arrives at his second-floor office. It is the classic two-room principal setup. Chad never uses the front room and its formidable rectangular metal desk, the kind every sinister principal sits behind in high school rom-com films. He prefers the more casual back room where he can talk to students and hold meetings at a round table.

Ever since he sent out a note to parents about the Monday night threat, he has received a steady stream of text messages and emails from concerned and fearful parents and staff. They want to know their children are safe. Chad keeps checking his phone, shooting off short reassuring answers. Leaning over the mini fridge in the corner, he pulls out a bag of deli turkey, avocado, and a sandwich baggie full of ranch dressing. He's trying the Keto Diet, the no sugar, no carb cleanse, which he's hoping will help him shed the weight he's gained since he took the job at Sullivan. When he decided to apply for the role, several people told him not to take it if he got an offer. Colleagues said the school was likely to close and Chad's career as a principal would end before it even got off the ground. But the fact that Sullivan was one of the worst-performing schools in the city didn't deter Chad, it motivated him. He considered himself a person who ran toward fire rather than away from it.

When Chad looks at his Sullivan ID, the image makes him laugh. He looks so young and sparkly eyed. The last five years have taken a toll.

Growing up in Mississippi, Chad changed schools almost every year. His father, an undercover narcotics officer, couldn't afford to stay in any one place long. His safety was always at risk. Chad remembered he had a collection of silk shirts worthy of Don Johnson's James Crockett on *Miami Vice*. The trunk of his father's unmarked car would sometimes be filled with machine guns. When he was working, Chad's father would disappear for days on end and when he'd return, he would bring Chad oversized necklaces with heavy, embossed images of cannabis leaves. Inevitably, after six months in any one town, Chad's father would announce that they were moving on. Chad credits his mother, who had Chad at nineteen, for raising him amid the chaos.

When Chad was twelve, his family arrived in Gulfport, Mississippi. There, Chad was selected to attend one of the state's first busing programs, an effort to desegregate schools across the state. Early each morning, Chad was bused to an almost entirely Black school on the north side of the city in time to be inside the school gates by 8 a.m. At 8:01 a.m., the gates were locked until the end of the school day. No one got in or out of the building until 3 p.m. Life inside the building, however, was worse for Chad than out. He was often cornered and beaten up. Trips to the bathroom usually guaranteed a pummeling. He had watches pulled from his wrist. Chad was also diagnosed with a learning disability midway through the year. He flunked the grade. That summer, Chad's family left Mississippi for good and moved to Indiana for a new start.

When Chad took the job as assistant principal at Harper High School in 2010, he knew the position would come with extreme academic and social challenges that would push him. His first day on the job, Chad watched as two boys tangled. Without thinking, Chad grabbed one of the boys and pulled him into a nearby classroom. Just as he managed to get inside the door, Chad saw a fist fly past him. Glass shattered everywhere and one boy landed a punch right in the other's face. The boy in the hallway had punched through the door's window. *Holy fuck*, Chad thought to himself, *what have I gotten myself into?*

But Chad soon learned that physical fights were symptoms of much deeper struggles. At Harper, students carried heavy burdens. Englewood was a place penetrated by pain. Trauma touched countless households in the South Side neighborhood, and living there meant enduring the corrosive effects of poverty and gun violence. Much of Chad's job at Harper was finding ways to help kids cope. But Chad also came to understand the limits of his position, a lesson that came with heartbreak.

One Harper student Chad still thinks about is Cedric. He tried to greet Cedric every day during lunch. Chad, the once-bullied kid, always found himself drawn to the outsiders. Cedric was a sweet, quiet freshman with a big smile and wire-frame glasses. Chad recalls the last time he saw Cedric alive. He waved to the boy as he sat in the cafeteria finishing his lunch. A week later, a policeman called to say a student had been shot and killed a block from school. That was a few days before spring break, and Chad was the only administrator on campus. He agreed to try to identify the body. It was Cedric on the concrete, in a pool of blood where he had been gunned down. Cedric's mother was leaning over him screaming. A police helicopter flew overhead looking for the shooters. Chad remembers the noise of the helicopter mixing with Cedric's mother's cries.

The police failed to identify or catch Cedric's killer. And over the next three years, more than fifty current and former Harper students were shot, nine of them killed. One morning, Chad witnessed a teen in a Batman suit riding a moped and spraying half a dozen people down with an Uzi. On another, he got out of his car to the sounds of two boys shooting into a crowd of students on the school blacktop. So much of Chad's job involved managing the trauma and fallout of students' experiences that he failed to notice his own.

By the time Chad started his job at Sullivan, he had developed post-traumatic stress disorder. He would see stains of red whenever he heard helicopters overhead. And there were those images of Cedric lying on the ground. They paralyzed him for minutes at a time. When he'd sit in his office, Chad would involuntarily jerk his neck backward. Later, he realized it was a habit he'd developed from hearing gunshots on a regular basis. Chad, it turns out, had not just come to Sullivan to turn the school around. Sullivan was also his chance to heal.

At Sullivan, Chad keeps a journal in an office desk drawer. Faded and buried under a pile of books, the pages pay homage to his students who have died from gun violence. The heightened threats at Sullivan have reminded him that he has a few names to add. None of them Sullivan students, thank goodness. Chad intends to keep it that way. But he knows better than most, that no matter how many drills or rules or peace circles he runs, the world doesn't stop at the doors of a school. Rather, the entire world seems to unfold inside of them. At Sullivan, refugee students share space with Chicago kids who fight to survive, too. Among them is a football star who started selling drugs at age eight when his mother could no longer afford to pay rent. Another, a buoyant senior alive with school spirit who has spent his life bouncing between dozens of foster homes. There are students who have seen friends gunned down and those who memorize Bible verses hoping they won't face a similar fate. So many Sullivan students bear witness to the tragic and the horrifically ugly. But, then again. February can be depressing.

8

MARCH

Alejandro

Alejandro hasn't heard from his mother, Luana, in five days. He's beginning to worry. Or, rather, he's beginning to worry more than usual. The two last spoke on Sunday before Alejandro left the house for a soccer game. Alejandro doesn't expect to speak to his mother every day. He often goes several days without hearing from her. Luana still lives in Guatemala City and can only communicate with her son when she has money to buy a bit of data on her mobile phone. Alejandro's father usually sends Luana money on the weekends, and some of that allows the two to text and video chat each other. The small amount of data tends to last a few days, depending on how many other phone calls Luana makes. Five days without any contact, however, is unusual.

Alejandro knows there are numerous reasons his mother might not be reachable. She may have lost her phone. Her neighborhood, Alejandro's old neighborhood, may be gripped by one of its occasional blackouts. She could have spent her data allowance calling other family members. Alejandro holds on to such reasons. If he lets his mind wander unchecked, his worries grow macabre.

Alejandro sits on the pullout futon couch in the living room, which doubles as a second bedroom. He has the main bedroom to himself while his father, Sergio, and his stepmother sleep on the unfolded couch at night. His gray shirt blends with the plaid comforter that covers the futon. As usual, a FIFA soccer game fills the large television that sits across from the couch. The match is not one that Alejandro is invested in. He mutes it. The small table between the bed and screen hold an array of condiments: ketchup, Cholula and tomatillo hot sauces, and a bottle of partially finished orange soda. The small desk where Alejandro does homework sits against the wall. Over it, on a calendar mounted on a small whiteboard, the senior has marked his graduation date with a bright blue circle. Two framed paper certificates celebrate Alejandro's top grades, earned at the end of his junior year. He wouldn't get one this term. He has let his grades slip. Alejandro unlocks his phone screen for the umpteenth time and looks for a sign of his mother. He sees the last conversation he had with Luana. It began the same way as hundreds of conversations the two have had over the last five years.

Good morning, son. How are you? Luana wrote.

Good morning, Alejandro responded.

I pray to God that you have a good day today, Luana continued. *I pray that no one hurts you. And I pray that you are suc-*

cessful in all you do. Your brother is sick. He hasn't been feeling well. My bones have been hurting, Son.

Alejandro knows the complaint his mother describes. When the temperature drops, his bones ache as though a bitter wind chill has settled in his marrow.

I haven't been feeling so good, either, Alejandro wrote. *I took some medicine at 2 a.m. I'm going to take more now.*

Son, you must eat something before you take medicine.

For the last five years, Luana has parented over text message. She texts to make sure he does his homework. She keeps tabs on his grades. Luana asks about Alejandro's girlfriend and if he scored at his most recent soccer match. She encourages him to go to bed at a reasonable hour and to limit the time he spends playing his FIFA video games.

What are you doing now? Luana continued.

I'm eating.

Luana also regularly asks Alejandro about graduation. He will be her first child to graduate from high school. Though she's twenty-eight hundred miles away, Luana wants to ensure that nothing prevents her son from walking across the stage. She knows that with just three months until graduation, Alejandro cannot afford any major missteps, not at school and not outside. Luana is not alone. Alejandro's father, his friends, the Sullivan teachers, and Alejandro himself all know that things that might be blips in another teenager's life could completely derail his future in the United States. Hopes are on him. Despite the distance between them, Alejandro knows that his mother already sees his graduation fully in her imagination. Why worry her with his dropping grades? News of his poor grades would hit her hard, even if it won't keep him from earning his diploma. Alejandro prefers not to burden his mother with bad news. The stakes are too high. He'd rather focus their conversations around helping Luana get to Chicago. If for no other reason, Alejandro intends to graduate high school and land a well-paying job so he can save up and buy Luana a house.

Recently, Luana has mentioned her dream of opening a restaurant in Guatemala City. That worries Alejandro. He wants his mother to have aspirations but starting a business there would almost surely require paying a fee to members of MS-13, whose dominance in Alejandro's home neighborhood has only grown. The group now commands large swaths of the city, using its numbers and ruthlessness to tighten its hold on businesses and residents. If Alejandro's mother opened a restaurant, they would demand extortion payments. And even if she paid them, it wouldn't guarantee his mother's safety. The cost of opening a restaurant in Guatemala, Alejandro told his mother, is too high. The cost of remaining in Guatemala, he thinks, is also too high.

But Alejandro still aches for his home. He keeps a stack of printed photos in his dresser. They are images from Guatemala. An early birthday party; a soccer game. One of his favorites depicts ten-year-old Alejandro looking up at the camera. He's shirtless and his hair is wet. He looks directly at the lens, mean-mugging the cameraman. He was skinny and small back then and he used to gel his black hair up and into a spiky triangle that protruded from the edge of his forehead. The photo was taken on a hot afternoon when Alejandro and his friends hiked to a river and spent the day swimming and lounging on its muddy banks. In Guatemala, Alejandro was rarely without his friends. Beginning at age five, he attached himself to a group of older boys who were like surrogate brothers. In a city where public trust in police and government was tenuous at best, Alejandro's friends not only offered a social network, but safety, too. The group always traveled as a pack. They'd play pickup soccer games in the neighborhood streets and competed in online FIFA games, too. The group would ride their bikes around the city, stopping for *hilachas*, stewed shredded beef served on the streets in giant vats, or beans and macaroni salad dished out in small Styrofoam containers.

The images transport Alejandro to sunny days in Guatemala, but they also remind him of how long ago they were. Those sun-drenched images are not the Guatemala he left behind. In the months before he fled, Alejandro watched as friends turned on one another. It grew increasingly hard to distinguish between those he could trust, and those who would use his trust to lure and pressure him into MS-13. And those who remained outside the gang didn't last long.

In his first couple years in the United States, Alejandro dreaded hearing from his mother. She had become a reporter of tragedy, and Alejandro feared that each message would bring news of another death.

Everything here is bad, Luana told Alejandro the first time he called her from the United States.

Why? Alejandro asked.

One of your friends got shot.

Who?

Puerco. They shot him four times in the abdomen. He'd been drinking and he started running. But he was losing blood quickly. Someone saw that he was bleeding and called an ambulance.

Puerco survived, but many of Alejandro's friends did not. Bad news kept coming. In one particularly brutal incident, Luana relayed that one of his friends had been dismembered into forty different parts. The police found pieces of his corpse when a neighbor found his dog digging up a partially decomposed hand.

By 2015, Luana had reported deaths of nearly ten of Alejandro's friends. Across Guatemala, the number of murders ticked upward. Some months, more than five hundred murders were recorded and year-end reports totaled nearly six thousand. Alejandro started to have recurring nightmares. He couldn't free himself from the terror even in his sleep. The distance didn't make Alejandro feel safe. It left him feeling hopeless. He thought to himself: *I don't have any more friends. In Guatemala or in America. I have no friends in Chicago and everyone at home is dying. I don't want to live no more.*

One morning before school, Alejandro opened the bathroom cabinet and found a bottle of NyQuil. He took as many pills as he could fit in his mouth. When he arrived at Sullivan, his girlfriend met him by the door. He saw two of her. He saw two of everything. Alejandro's girlfriend rushed him to the school clinic where the nurse called an ambulance. He spent a week in the hospital and several more in intensive therapy. His therapist gave him techniques to deal with the stress of bad news. One included a stress ball, which the therapist told Alejandro to squeeze when he felt engulfed by anger or despair. He still has the dense blue ball. He stores it on his dresser, just a few inches above his stack of photos.

Alejandro pulls himself off the futon bed and returns to his text conversation with Luana. She still hasn't written to him. His eyes settle on the final messages in their last exchange. Luana had signed off with familiar words of encouragement, the same ones she told Alejandro the day he fled to the United States: *God takes care of those who are good. You are good.*

Sarah Quintenz

Abdul Karim, a Syrian senior, storms into the ELL office. He sits down next to Danny Rizk, who has spent the last several minutes eyeing a pair of the Air Jordan 1 shoes on a streetwear resale site. He's a sneakerhead.

"I'm so sick of this," Abdul Karim says, agitated. "Why do

some people always think Arab boys are bad? I'm not bad. They don't know me."

"Honestly?" Danny says looking up from his phone. "It's not worth your energy to dwell on things people say."

"But some people, they hate Arab students," Abdul Karim continues. "Why they hate us? That's called discrimination."

"Look, you are going to face discrimination the rest of your life in America," Danny continues. "It's gonna suck."

"But when I came to America they told me, 'Welcome to free country.'"

"Let me give you a new welcome," Danny says, now turning toward Abdul Karim. "Welcome to a lie."

Across the table, Sarah is immersed in another world. She must address the grim news delivered to her by Matt Fasana earlier in the week. The additional Chicago Public Schools funding, which remains dependent on new refugee students enrolling at Sullivan, is in danger of being eliminated. While Sullivan received a record number of new refugee students in 2017, President Trump has since introduced new, severe restrictions on refugee resettlements in the United States. The measures have already cut the number so severely that Sullivan has enrolled just one-fifth as many refugee students as it did in recent years. Sarah must now make the case to OLCE, the department that doles out the federal funds allocated for schools who serve foreign-born students, that Sullivan deserves a second lump sum to keep its burgeoning program alive.

Losing the OLCE funding would be devastating. If the department does not renew the funds, Sarah will likely have to lay off several of the staff she just hired, a few of whom left well-paying jobs because they believed in Sullivan's mission to serve refugee students. It would likely mean losing Danny, who fields queries and concerns like Abdul Karim's on a daily basis. Losing funds to staff Danny alone could have a withering effect on Sullivan's ELL program.

For Sarah, losing the funding means rolling back years of work. Ever since Chad put Sarah in charge of the ELL program in 2013, Sarah, along with Matt Fasana, has dug in to reshape it. After she introduced the "cohort" model, a classroom structure where students learn in pods determined by their mastery of English, Sarah and Matt also made sure to get word out to the five major resettlement agencies and establish better communication with them. The two spent hours in meetings, pushing the message that Sullivan High School would be *the* Chicago high school for refugee students.

But Sarah's case to OLCE must be a pragmatic one. The head of the department has asked her to prepare a one-page report that he can review at the next meeting. Sarah has enlisted Annmarie Handley, who has experience in marketing and grant writing, to help make a case for the program. She'll then present the language to Matt who may well end up presenting the flyer to OLCE. Bureaucracy.

Annmarie sits just inches away from Sarah at the office table. Both women have their laptops open.

"I feel like when we're talking about our mission, we should focus on the English language program, because that's what we're giving the kids," says Annmarie, who points to some initial language she's written for the presentation. "It's under the umbrella of this Newcomer Center that is part of Sullivan High School."

Sarah nods and adds an *mm-hmm*, in agreement.

"So, I think we should start with what we have done with that money," Annmarie continues. "You said we got two years' worth of money. We need to tell them we went from *this* to *this*. And how that's different from other schools. Why do we deserve that money more than other programs?"

Annmarie throws out an idea. She and Sarah could design the page with a graphic that mimics the design of drugstore medicine bottles. One side of the graphic, she explains, should show what Sullivan has accomplished, while the other shows other CPS high schools such as Mather and Senn. "It should make it really easy to look at and see that we have more refugee and immigrant students than them."

Sullivan, for one, doesn't just boast more refugee students. Mather has just two dedicated ELL teachers and Senn has gone years with none at all. New student enrollment at both schools can prove long and arduous, and several refugee students have complained that administrative staff pay little to no attention to their particular needs.

Annmarie then turns to the working mission statement of their program. *We are the English Language Program for Sullivan High School Newcomer Center.* The language gives Sarah pause.

"See, here's where I get caught up. A Newcomer Center, I've never liked that name," she says. The ELL program rebrand remains a work in progress.

"I don't like it either," Annmarie adds.

"Well, let's get rid of it. No more Newcomer Center. This is the International Academy at Sullivan High School."

Over the years, Sarah has collected and mastered a set of facts about the ELL program, or International Academy. If asked, she can provide data points on the spot: thirty-five countries, thirty-eight languages, and more than three hundred students who have participated in ELL classes. Numbers like these can fit easily on a one-page document and, hopefully, compel attention. But Sarah keeps a second set of data in her head, too. One less easily measured by standard metrics. It includes the time when Sarah left a laundry basket out and offered to wash students' uniforms. Many of them cannot afford to wash their clothes at the neighborhood laundromat. There is the period of time she found herself at the DMV almost once each week in order to help a group of Syrian students apply for driver's permits, and she needed to help them navigate Illinois's vetting process, which took longer for Syrian refugees than for others. And there are the hours she's spent on her students' informal Americanization, such as teaching them to trick-or-treat for their first Halloweens. One year, she had her students organize themselves in a single-file line outside her classroom door, and one by one they approached Sarah and said, "Trick or treat," before Sarah handed them a piece of candy.

Sarah has learned that seemingly simple things, like how to use an apartment doorbell, must be learned anew. She taught this particular lesson after she'd heard students had been throwing rocks at their neighbors' windows. These important data points are hard to quantify. She can no longer keep count of times she's sat down with students to show them how to pay bills. Or when, after discovering her students dating for the first time, she gives them impromptu sex education lessons.

"Don't let your boyfriend make you feel bad for telling him to wear a condom," she'll tell the girls. "And if you're too embarrassed to openly discuss safe sex, then you're not ready to have sex."

Because much of Sarah's goal for the students is to make them feel safe and happy, the numbers that ultimately matter are often the bad things that didn't happen, and the ones beyond a tally.

Also incalculable are the ways Sarah's students have left an indelible mark on her. Like when a few days before Sarah's thirty-seventh birthday, her students organized a surprise party for her. Just before the class period was supposed to begin, Sarah was called to the music room at the opposite end of the hall. With Sarah out of the room, her students scurried to decorate.

"Everyone put your food on the desks," a senior girl instructed. Soon, the room was transformed into an international feast. Bowls of hummus, trays of chicken curry and peanut noodles, *fufu*, pico de gallo, and a spread of Middle Eastern salads topped a collection of desks pushed to the middle of the room. Several students brought liter bottles of Diet Coke and piled them in a corner. Another provided a store-bought cake with "Happy Birthday Ms. Q" written in frosting across the top. Once the food was out, the same senior told everyone to write "Happy Birthday" in their native languages on the whiteboard.

Joyeux anniversaire.

Eid milad saeid.

Heri ya sikukuu ya kuzaliwa.

Eleven different languages filled the board. The group then huddled at the back of the room and dimmed the lights. They each held a corner of a hand-drawn banner that read "Happy Birthday Ms. Q!" in multicolored letters. When Sarah entered the room, the group cheered. The senior stage manager cued up a playlist of Sarah's favorite songs including Justin Bieber's "Love Yourself," a tune she'd played for the students dozens of times. Midway through the party, a group of girls handed Sarah a thick book made from construction paper and held together by string. Sarah grasped it carefully with both hands.

The title: "Ms. Q Travels the World." Each student had drawn Sarah a picture. They were images and descriptions of the students' home countries. *She would drink jasmine tea*, one page read with an image of a small streetscape from Homs, Syria.

She would see giraffes and zebras, read another written by a Kenyan student who accompanied the words with pictures of the animals.

The book brought Sarah to tears. Its pages were not just an imagined travelogue, but a document of what was lost to violence and war in the students' communities, a time capsule of their crumbled worlds.

The students could pull Sarah up when she was low. A year before Sarah's surprise party, her students collected around her as her own world fell apart. Sarah had just separated from her then-husband and the decision to break apart her family left her shattered. She took a leave of absence from Sullivan. She needed to spend time with her son, then just five, and mend from the heartbreak. The decision was not an easy one for Sarah. But she knew if she couldn't show up as the best version of herself, it was better to step away. Midway through her leave of absence, a colleague reported that Sarah's students wanted an update on her well-being. Sarah agreed to visit them. When she arrived at her classroom, her students swarmed her. Sarah asked everyone to sit in a circle on the floor. She sat down with them and held up a piece of paper.

"You know when a man and woman love each other, they

get married, right?" Sarah said as she drew stick figures of a woman and man holding hands inside a circle.

Her students nodded. "Well, sometimes, that love changes and in America, men and women go through something called divorce." Sarah paused to draw an "X" through the circle. "A divorce means you're no longer married."

The students remained silent. For many, dissolution of marriage came only in death, or when a husband repudiates his wife. The notion that a man and woman would together decide to end a marriage was new.

"I need time to heal myself," Sarah continued. "And I need time to heal my family."

"Can we pray for you?" one student asked without raising his hand.

"Yes, you can pray for me," Sarah said. "Everyone. Hugs."

Sarah pulled herself up from the floor. As she did, her students formed a line in front of her. One by one, they hugged her. Some only let go when classmates peeled them off. Some she knew to fist-bump while others gave brief hugs, their shoulders barely touching Sarah's. As the line shortened, a Somali sophomore made her way to the front. Standing at barely five feet, she held her hands up and hovered them an inch away from Sarah's temples. Closing her eyes, she whispered a prayer in Somali. When she finished, she opened her eyes and looked directly at Sarah.

"You will heal," she said in English. "God will heal you."

The final layout of Sarah and Annmarie's flyer for OLCE spreads across two pages. The first page features a panel with Sullivan's yellow *S* insignia and a world map beneath it. The second highlights the ELL program's mission, a goal described in educational jargon that points toward making students good citizens. Sarah understands that this version will most effectively deliver her message up the CPS ladder. If she had her way, however, the mission might read: *To help students feel like they are a part of this country; that America is their country. To share the motto: If we're not laughing, we're crying. And to help them feel secure and content and teach them to always wear a condom.*

Mariah

Mariah keeps her eyes on a group of Syrian and Afghani refugee boys in the corner of the room. She doesn't want them to approach her and her pointed glare makes her aim clear. Mariah is not wearing her uniform today. Not disobedience this time—she says she put those days behind her—but because Chad recently introduced dress-down Fridays at Sullivan. No uniforms required. Outside, the remaining mounds of snow have turned to a grayish slush. The sun has emerged from a long winter hibernation, casting a yellow glow on the otherwise gloomy streetscape. Inside Sullivan, however, spring fully blooms. The halls are bouncing. Girls in skinny white jeans paired with cropped floral tops mingle with others in faded pants with pre-torn cuts across the knees. Sneakers skid across the floors, emitting high-pitched squeaks that echo throughout the halls. Boys in tapered sweatpants and fitted T-shirts tucked beneath hoodie sweatshirts nod to one another in recognition. The drab down jackets have given way to brighter ones. There's an audible brightness in students' voices and a slight bounce in their gait. The winter lull has begun to lift.

Mariah has picked one of her favorite pairings for dress-down Friday: light blue jeans ripped at the knees, of course, plus a plain T-shirt, and a zip-up hoodie, open to reveal her straightened hair. The sophomore knows her mother would kill her if she caught her daughter in this outfit, and so she hides the jeans in her school locker.

Mariah settles into a chair toward the center of the library. She continues to eye the group of Arabic-speaking boys. One of them, a smaller Syrian boy with bright green eyes and a confident, impish edge, notices. He saunters over to her.

"I swear to God you are Arab," he says to her in English.

Mariah stares back at him. She does not respond.

The boy looks over his shoulder and repeats the sentiment to his friends in Arabic. "I know she is Arab."

Mariah holds her ground. She says nothing. This isn't the first time this group of boys has approached her. Earlier this winter, one of the boys overheard a cafeteria line cook ask Mariah in Arabic what she'd like for lunch. The boy turned to Mariah then and asked, with shock and delight, if she was Arab. Mariah ignored him. She had eavesdropped on the boys and heard them making lewd comments about classmates and school staff. They'd call girls and bare-shouldered teachers *waqiha*, a crass, derogatory term for women. For Mariah, the group represents the worst of Muslim men. Judgmental, sexist, and rude. She thinks of her cousin, who dropped out at seventeen, and would be a senior at Sullivan if she hadn't had an arranged marriage and two babies. The too real possibility that Mariah's parents might eventually arrange for her to marry such a man depresses the sophomore.

At home, Mariah's life is ruled by strict expectations. The apartment seems to be always full with the comings and goings of Mariah's siblings, cousins, nieces, nephews, and neighbors. The living room at the front of the apartment is lined with big, overstuffed couches that form a horseshoe around a large flat-screen television. When Mariah's father, brothers, and uncles are home, usually between shifts at work, they tend to congregate there. Gray stains dot the cream-colored carpet, remnants of long nights the men spend over the hookah. Mariah's mother, Fatmeh, and her sisters often squeeze altogether in the small kitchen, where a stove butts up against a sink and an ever-growing pile of dishes and Tupperware. Fatmeh churns out massive spreads of halal dishes. One favorite is *margat alb-amiya*, a mixture of baked okra and tender lamb that she lays over spiced rice or sometimes over dolma, finger-length rolls of minced meat, rice, and nuts wrapped in chard and dusted with lemon zest. She fries falafel and makes spinach and feta pies. As far as Mariah is concerned, her mother's cooking is second to none. When they can escape their chores, the girls retreat to their room where they watch *How to Get Away with Murder* on their school-issued laptops. When Fatmeh does enlist Mariah to help cook and clean, Mariah often shirks the tasks. She resents not only the chores but also that her brothers don't have to do them. When Mariah complains, however, Fatmeh offers the same response.

"This is not confidence, this is rudeness," Fatmeh tells her daughter. "When you get married, how will you deal with your husband? He will want to leave you because you will not respect him."

The idea infuriates Mariah. *We live in America*, she thinks to herself. *We should just get used to it here because we're never going back to Iraq. That's a fact.*

Mariah, who left Iraq at age ten, has very few memories of Basra, the coastal, port city where she was born. When she is not locked in a familial battle, she likes to revisit the parts of her life that she does recall and talk about them with her mother. Such reminiscences can happen any time, such as when they're relaxed together on the big red couch.

"I remember that someone would come around with gas tanks, and you'd have to give them an empty one to get a new one," Mariah says to Fatmeh in a typical exchange, speaking of the liquid natural gas the family used to heat its stove and oven. "I would roll the tanks because I couldn't carry them."

The scene makes Fatmeh laugh.

"Even water," Fatmeh adds. "We had to buy water to drink."

"'Cause there was salt in the water that came out of the sink."

"Salt, yes."

"And then for the water, there was this big red thing that water goes in and it's like for the whole house."

"Yes, a tank."

"It got to be on top of the bathroom. We had to buy one. Remember?"

"Yeah, I do."

"I was always scared to go inside the bathroom because it was outside the house. The roof was broken and I was always scared that it was going to fall on top of my head."

Mariah and Fatmeh's conversations can go on like this for over an hour. Mariah recalling small details, Fatmeh confirming them. For Mariah, revisiting the images is more like reviewing a plot of a movie she saw long ago. For Fatmeh such conversations can leave her longing for Iraq.

But the nostalgia comes to an end for Mariah when her mother holds her to old-world expectations. Mariah knows the steps of an arranged marriage; she's seen several of her siblings and cousins follow them. First, Fatmeh will invite Mariah's potential future mother-in-law over to the apartment. The two mothers will sit in the family living room to talk and Mariah will be reluctantly glued to the red pleather sofa to observe. Fatmeh will offer a plate of dried and fresh fruits. She'll brew tea and serve it in their best pot and cups. Fatmeh will watch Mariah closely, sending her invisible signals to sit up and smile; she will encourage her daughter to be polite and demure. If Mariah behaves—no mentions of Snapchat, or steamy *Riverdale* stars, and certainly not her decision to remove her hijab—the mothers will plan to introduce their children.

Mariah can't help but fantasize about another kind of courtship, one that might start in the bleachers at a Sullivan Tigers basketball game. There, Mariah would sit and watch a player she's dated for several months. The boy, who is funny and athletic, celebrates her independence. Mariah could sit with her mother and introduce her to classmates and their parents. They could cheer on the Tigers and laugh about prom and their favorite Auntie Anne's dipping sauce. But Mariah knows such wishful thinking will remain exactly that, so she tries not to let herself disappear into such fantasies. Instead, every time her older sister Farha, now several months pregnant with her first child, calls to speak with Fatmeh, Mariah peppers her with the same set of questions, perhaps hoping to one day get an answer that will give her reasons to look forward to the married life their mother almost certainly has planned for her.

"What do you think of marriage?" Mariah asks Farha.

"It's not the best decision to make," her sister answers. "But it's not the wrong one. There's good stuff about it and there's bad stuff."

"Well, at least you're happy," Mariah will say, unsure how to digest her sister's response.

"Yeah."

FATMEH

•

Mariah was born in Basra, Iraq, on the eve of the Iraq War, a war propelled by President George W. Bush's announcement of his "global war on terrorism" and the decision to overthrow Saddam Hussein. Fatmeh was living with six children, when in 2003, the British military took Basra by force in a storm of shells and tank fire. On nights when Fatmeh heard bombs overhead, she'd tell her children to hide beneath the stairs while she gathered the few sacks of flour she had and arranged the bags into a small barrier around them. Every time the blast cracked in the hot desert air her children would scream. Fatmeh prayed. *Allah, please look after us,* she would say. *Keep us all safe.*

Basra was no longer the city it once was. It had long stood as one of the country's most handsome, verdant urban centers, a lush cityscape dotted with towering date palms, pastel-painted buildings and wood-carved balconies, lime orchards, and a central waterway that carried water from the Tigris and Euphrates Rivers to the Persian Gulf.

Fatmeh, herself Kuwaiti, arrived in Basra with her husband, Khalil, in 1991. Khalil's family was from the region, though Khalil himself had grown up in Kuwait. Khalil and Fatmeh, then just twenty, had imagined raising their children in Kuwait, but the Persian Gulf War, which ignited when Iraq, under Saddam Hussein's rule, invaded the smaller neighboring country in hopes of seizing its oil wells, eroded their hopes for such a future. The invasion left much of Kuwait in shambles. By the time Fatmeh, Khalil, and their four young children crossed the border into Iraq, nearly half of Kuwait's population had fled the country. In Basra, Fatmeh, who felt like an outsider, found herself trying to build a life in a broken city.

The once-opulent Basra landscape had been decimated by the near decade-long war between Iran and Iraq. A failed uprising against Saddam Hussein had also left tens of thousands dead. But Basra wasn't just plagued by war and political upheaval. Like the rest of Iraq, the city had also been throttled by sanctions, which the United Nations Security Council imposed to punish Iraq for invading Kuwait. The embargo prevented countries from trading with Iraq except for limited amounts of food, medicine, and other relief aids. For Basra, a place that depended almost entirely on imported food, the sanctions could be felt in every facet of life.

Like so many mothers, Fatmeh fought every day to defend her children against the hunger that afflicted the country. By 1995, more than three hundred thousand Iraqi children had died due to steeply rising malnutrition and shortages in medical supplies. Deaths related to diarrheal disease had more than tripled across the country as water sanitation systems deteriorated and hospitals functioned with limited staff. Every morning Fatmeh, not yet thirty with five young children, would wake up in her apartment, a crowded place that she shared with her in-laws, and ask herself the same question: *How will I get bread today?*

Piece by piece, Fatmeh sold nearly every bit of gold jewelry she had received as wedding gifts ten years earlier. When she ran out of bracelets and necklaces, she began to sell her own clothes. Several small markets had sprung up around Basra where residents would sell pieces of their lives. Fatmeh sold her shoes and dresses until she had only one tunic remaining. She never bought herself a second one—whatever money she made from her sales she'd spend on her children.

Between the money she made from selling her belongings and some pocket money her family in Kuwait sent on occasion, Fatmeh managed to keep her children healthy. But she was haunted by the deaths of other young people. There was one girl in particular she could not forget: While visiting a neighbor in the hospital, Fatmeh passed a hospital room where a young girl lay on a propped-up hospital bed. A yellow IV was attached to her arm. The girl's eyes were shut, but Fatmeh could tell she was beautiful. The room smelled of death, but Fatmeh watched as the doctors and nurses wrote down notes in their charts as calmly as if they were writing a grocery list. *We are used to death*, Fatmeh thought to herself.

After Saddam Hussein was removed from power in 2003, Khalil took a job with the U.S. military working as a security guard at a base that had been set up in As-Salam Palace, a former home of the fallen Iraqi president. Not long after he started the job, a neighbor knocked on the door. When Fatmeh answered, he told her that he had been approached by four men looking for her husband. Fatmeh did not know who the men were. They could have been Sunni supporters of Saddam Hussein or from the Mahdi Army, the anti-U.S. Shia militia who sought to restore

Iraqi sovereignty. Or perhaps it was a local gang. No matter who the men were, they had delivered a clear warning: Was Khalil afraid to die? He was told to quit his job with the U.S. military or be killed.

Fatmeh heard rumors of kill lists that named Iraqi citizens who worked for the United States. One of Khalil's colleagues was kidnapped and murdered for his work on the U.S. base. She feared her husband was next. At night, she would bring her children to the roof where they would sleep while she and Khalil watched the street below. *They will come*, she thought to herself. *They will come and they will kill us.*

When Khalil eventually resigned from his post, he used what little savings he had to buy a taxi. Every time he left the house, however, Fatmeh feared her husband would not return. Khalil was often trailed by men on motorbikes and Fatmeh spotted cars parked outside their home. In 2007, they sold the taxi. Driving wasn't safe.

Life in Basra was no longer tenable. Khalil and his two eldest sons fled for Jordan on a tourist visa and applied for refugee status with the United Nations. He described to a U.N. representative a life of fear. Only one percent of refugees are selected for resettlement in new countries and once approved, refugees have no say in where they end up. By 2010, there were nearly two million Iraqi refugees alone. But Khalil got lucky. He was approved in 2010 and resettled in Chicago that same year.

Khalil told Fatmeh to wait in Basra until he saved enough money to care for his family in Chicago. It took three years. By the time she left Iraq, Fatmeh had spent two decades scrambling through the rubble of a country ripped apart by war. When Fatmeh stepped through the doorframe of her Basra home for the last time, her house stood empty. Tears filled her eyes. Chicago would eventually be a place where her children, and grandchildren, would grow up. In Chicago, her children would graduate from high school, and some would even go on to college. It would be a place where she'd find Iraqi traditions pitted against American teenage life. She'd learn to speak English, come to love Snapchat, and eventually apply for and be granted American citizenship. But there, in her entranceway, Fatmeh considered how she hadn't chosen America. She hadn't chosen Basra, either. Home was a notion scattered over time, and a place long faded. But soon, she hoped, America would feel something like it.

9

APRIL

Shahina

"We need to figure out what the hell is going on with Sha-hina," says Sarah, looking up from her laptop. Several teachers have reported that the Burmese sophomore is close to failing their classes. While much of Sarah's fight to keep Sullivan's ELL program afloat rests on recruiting new students, she also needs to keep those already enrolled engaged in school. Some students who graduate from the ELL program do so with impressive scholarships to institutions such as University of Illinois–Chicago and Northeastern Illinois University. Others leave and find jobs to support their families. For Sarah, what matters most is ensuring students earn their diploma.

Sarah and the others also know that for some of the girls in the program, a sudden dip in their performance signals that they are being overwhelmed by pressures at home, sometimes so intense that they eventually disappear from school alto-gether. By now, Sarah knows the signals well and it's one of the struggles she takes most to heart. Add to that the practi-cal consideration that with only two months left to the school year, it's a race against the clock. For Shahina's sake, certainly. Also, for the health of the ELL program and its funding. Its overseers at CPS look closely at whether students show up. "Her attendance is hovering at thirty percent," Sarah reports.

"I think she wants us to call her Serena," says Fatima Peters, looking up at Sarah. This is Fatima's first year as one of Sullivan's full-time ELL tutors. "She told me last week. I think she's trying to be more American. Did you see her at Report Card Pick-Up? She came without her hijab. It seems like she's going through some kind of identity crisis."

"I've heard rumors about an arranged marriage," Sarah tells Fatima. "Sometimes girls show up less and less until one day you find out they're married and living in Phoenix, with a forty-year-old guy and his dad."

"Arizona? For real?" asks Fatima.

"I bet the nuns never prepared you for anything like that," says Sarah, getting up from her chair. Fatima came to Sullivan after a decade at a private Catholic school. "Not that anything can prepare you for these conversations."

Sarah, in search mode, first checks for Shahina in the first-floor girls' bathroom. Nassim, camera around his neck, stands a few feet away in a stairwell. He's huddled with a Black American boy, a classmate with whom he has grown inseparable. They travel the halls together, snapping photos of classmates. They've also developed their own signature handshakes, each of which includes intricate patterns of snaps and dabs. Nassim waves enthusiastically to Sarah. He hasn't been to the "womb" recently. These days, he spends more time in the digital media room, a third-floor space that attracts a tight-knit tribe of outsiders including Lauren. In the years following, Nassim will go on to sing Mariah Carey karaoke and inspire a short film loosely based on his life. He'll count *The Steve Harvey Show* among his favorite television programs and share once deeply buried stories about the tragedies he witnessed in the Syrian war. By sophomore year, Nassim will enjoy playing the role of seasoned student and will offer guidance to Sullivan newcomers. He'll continue to fall in and out of love, too. But for now, on the school stairs, heartbreak doesn't seem to weigh on the freshman today.

Shahina is not in the bathroom, so Sarah returns to the library. There, she finds the girl hidden beneath a table in the back corner of the room. Seeing Shahina hidden in shadow is a reminder of the library's many purposes: while Belenge came to these tables to confront his distress, Shahina now uses the same surfaces for cover.

Shahina's naturally round face is sharpened by thick, painted eyebrows, and narrowed by the poly-blend pashmina she fashions into a hijab. She's tucked in a tiny ball under the computer desks, her knees pulled into her chest. She seems relaxed. Beside her sits her closest friend, Aishah. The two are inseparable, gossiping and giggling everywhere they go. Like many refugee girls who find themselves alienated from their parents, Shahina and Aishah have become each other's chosen family.

At first, Sarah treads lightly. She asks Shahina if she's eaten and if she'd care to share her lunch. The Sullivan cafeteria serves three meals a day, but the kitchen is not halal, so some Muslim refugee students skip all three. Not just during Ramadan, but all year. Most don't bring their own lunches, either. Shahina smiles and shakes her head. Sarah pushes forward. She asks Shahina why she's been ditching school.

Shahina explains that she needs a job to pay back the man she was supposed to marry last year. Sarah's heart sinks, but she doesn't show it. Almost exactly one year ago, Shahina tells Sarah, her mother and stepfather sent her to Atlanta, Georgia, to marry a man named Hamid, almost ten years her senior. When Shahina made it clear she had no intention of marrying him, the wedding was called off. Now, she explains, she has to help pay back the $2,000 Hamid's family paid her mother as an engagement gift.

Sarah takes a deep breath. These stories never get easier to stomach. They are in direct contrast to everything Sarah stands for. And she knows Shahina's minute-long version leaves out a lot, but even Sarah could not have predicted the harrowing forced journey that saddled now seventeen-year-old Shahina with a debt so huge it dragged her out of school.

Shahina had just turned sixteen when her mother first brought Hamid, another Burmese refugee, to their family's apartment. Shahina's mother, Zakiah, told her Hamid was twenty-two, though he was really twenty-seven. A slight small man, Hamid wore a diamond stud, which Shahina figured was fake, and kept his glistening hair gelled back. Shahina, who sleeps on the couch of her family's three-room apartment, had cleared her duffle bags of clothes and dirty towels from the room and sat quietly as two of her three younger siblings ran around the room.

By refugee standards, Hamid had money. His family owned their own house and managed a Pakistani restaurant in Atlanta. Zakiah believed Hamid could take care of Shahina. She told her daughter she'd never want for anything with Hamid. Zakiah, who grew up in a wealthy family in Myanmar, knew how brutally fast bad luck can reverse one's station and the shock and pain of the poverty that can follow. Hamid wouldn't be perfect insurance, she told Shahina, but he was good for her and the family.

Hamid kept his distance from Shahina, only gazing at her from across the room.

"He is too short, and his skin was bad," Shahina later told her mother. "I cannot marry him."

Zakiah implored her daughter to reconsider. She said she was sick, possibly terminally, and she wanted to ensure that Shahina would be cared for if she died. Shahina suspected her mother was lying. She often feels her mother manipulates the facts. Shahina does, too, a pattern that both Sarah and Josh have noticed in the girl. Josh recognizes the behavior as one often seen in trauma victims. They are often skillful liars; the habit can help victims cope with PTSD. He's seen how it plays out across generations among the refugee families connected to the school. Then again, refugee or not, teens do sometimes mislead adults, and the teachers know that, too.

Zakiah's telling Shahina that she suffered a deadly illness might have been a lie, but the tactic worked. Shahina agreed to the engagement, if Hamid could wait until she finished high school to marry her. That would make it nearly a four-year engagement.

A week later, on Friday night after prayers, Zakiah hosted a celebratory henna night. Women and a few of Shahina's friends spent the night singing, eating, and painting intricate henna patterns on the newly betrothed girl's right hand and arm. When it's just women and girls, they can doff their hijabs and dote on each other's hair, too. Zakiah gave Shahina a ruby red dress with silver thread stitched across the collar and down the center. The dress, which draped far below Shahina's ankles, was paired with a silver headpiece and chiffon veil. Once Shahina was zipped in, Zakiah started on her daughter's makeup. She glued dense, long fake eyelashes to her lids and spread a thick layer of foundation across her face, patting it into her skin. Zakiah then brushed on two colors of blush and painted her lips with bright red lipstick. She pinned Shahina's hair into a beehive and with nearly half a can of hairspray made it feel like rigid wool.

Shahina barely moved from the couch the entire night. While her friends and family danced around her, singing along to their favorite pop songs, the girl wept, smearing the black mascara, foundation, and blush across her face. Her friends laughed. Looking at the pictures later, they told Shahina she looked like a "sad-ass monkey."

A couple weeks later, Hamid came to Chicago to take Shahina to Atlanta for a few days. It was Shahina's spring break, and she was supposed to just go for a visit. Her mother said she would trail Shahina and Hamid in her own car. But Zakiah never left Chicago. Only Shahina and Hamid would make the trip.

Hamid is Kaman, a member of a small Muslim minority centered in northern Myanmar. He spent most of the ride south speaking over the phone in a dialect that Shahina could not understand. When they arrived in Atlanta, Hamid parked and then immediately ushered Shahina to a small room in the basement of the house. She asked for the WiFi password and plopped herself on the bed. Out the small basement window she saw a cow roaming the large backyard. She turned to Facebook. After a few minutes, Halima, a friend from Myanmar who now lived in Atlanta with her parents, messaged her.

Congratulations on your wedding! So excited for Friday!

Girl, what are you talking about? Shahina wrote back. *I'm just here visiting, I'm not getting married.*

Halima sent her a picture of the wedding invitation. *It came in the mail last week*, she wrote. *And they already bought the cow to butcher for the wedding.*

Shahina sat in stunned silence. She started to cry. She had been conned into her own wedding. *This wasn't just trickery,* she thought. *This was kidnapping.*

Shahina wondered if this was punishment for being her father's daughter. When she was not yet two and Zakiah just twenty-seven, her father left them. Shahina barely remembers him. One constant, though incomplete reminder comes from her mother. Whenever Shahina pushes back against Zakiah, out pour her mother's curses against his name. Shahina imagines her stubbornness comes from her father. Among Burmese Muslims, women left by their husbands are counted as divorcées, and once her husband left, Zakiah was a pariah to marriageable men in her class. Used goods, bad luck, expensive to keep. These were all labels Zakiah wanted Shahina to avoid.

Locked in the basement, Shahina needed to come up with a plan—and quickly. The next day, Wednesday, two days before the planned wedding, she told Hamid she wanted to go home.

She explained that she was lonely and she missed her mother. She did not reveal she knew about the wedding. Hamid told her they would take her back to Chicago on Sunday, at the end of her spring break. "Just wait," he said.

Shahina stayed in her room, staring up at the ceiling from her futon bed. Her thoughts spiraled as she imagined one hellish future after another with the man who had bought her, stole her, and now locked her up. If she didn't find a way to escape Hamid's house, she'd be stuck here, cooking and cleaning for his entire family. Shahina thought of her classmate, an Iraqi girl who, when she got married, promised she would still finish high school. She said nothing would change. A few months later, the girl was pregnant and no longer attending school.

The looming possibility that Shahina would be confined to a similar life made her want to die. How was this life that her mother had forced upon her going to be any better than the one they fled in Myanmar? Shahina's life had been good there. Now, her mother intended to marry her off to a man who, though a refugee himself, was willing to humiliate, torment, and bully her. She was terrified. *A life with this kind of man*, Shahina thought, *was not a life worth living*. She began to consider the different ways she could kill herself. She could drink the contents of Hamid's medicine cabinet. She could bury her face in the pillow until she suffocated. If she could sneak past Hamid, his parents, and the growing number of cousins who had begun showing up, she could get a knife from the kitchen and slit her wrists. Shahina kept playing those images in her mind. In the end, she stayed put on the bed and waited.

Later that afternoon, Halima and her older brother came by to check in on Shahina. But before they could greet her, Hamid turned them away at the door. "Just leave her alone," Shahina heard him say from the next room. "Don't bother her."

Furious, Shahina waited until Hamid's parents came home. As soon as she heard their footsteps, she shouted, "I'm not going to marry your son! You cannot make me. Take me back to Chicago. If you don't, I'm calling the police."

"We're not taking you back," Hamid's mother retorted. "You agreed to marry our son."

Shahina, who often fought with her mother at home, knew what was coming next. Hamid would turn off the WiFi. Without internet, Shahina, who did not have a SIM card for her phone, would not be able to communicate with Halima—or anyone. Typing as fast as she could, Shahina sent a message to Halima, whose family was both wealthier and more permissive than Shahina's.

I need a SIM card, she wrote. *Come to my bedroom window later tonight. I will have money.*

Just past 4 a.m., Shahina heard a soft tapping on her window. It was Halima. She had the SIM card for her phone.

"Take this," Halima said. "Text me. I'm going to help you get out of here."

The two spent the rest of the night hatching a plan over text messages. Halima and her brother would come at breakfast time tomorrow and drive Shahina back to Chicago.

When Hamid came to her that morning, Shahina told him she was going home.

"You cannot leave," he repeated. "You stayed at my house. Everyone is going to think you're not a virgin. If you leave, everyone will think you're a whore."

"I don't give a damn what people think," Shahina said. "Let me leave."

Hamid tried to block the door.

Shahina ran to the kitchen and took a steak knife from the sink. She rolled up her left sleeve and started cutting small incisions on her wrist and inner arm. As she cut, she bellowed: "I'm going to kill myself in this kitchen if you do not let me go." This alarmed Hamid and his parents. He told Shahina she could go. "You owe us $2,000," he said.

Shahina ran out the door and called Halima. "Come get me now," she sobbed.

It took eleven hours to drive back to Chicago. In that time span, Hamid sent Shahina three dick pictures. The pictures disturbed Shahina, but they were certainly proof that she was right: he would not have been a good husband. When Shahina got home, her mother met her with disgust.

"You cannot come back here," Zakiah asserted. "If you come in here, I will not speak to you. You disgraced me."

"Mama, if you don't let me in, I'm calling the police," Shahina responded. She did not wait for an answer and pushed her way through the door. She'd learned about the police from American movies and overhearing Sarah tell another student to do precisely the same thing if they found themselves in danger.

While Shahina's fight impresses Sarah, the girl's story also leaves her head spinning. In her years of teaching inside Chicago Public Schools, she has seen all kinds of kids come in battered and bruised, others who have gone without food for days at a time, and countless students who have lost friends and family to violence. But, in Sarah's eyes, nothing orphans a teenage student from the hopes of a bright future in quite the same way as a forced marriage. Growing up, Sarah's step-father, a career military man and primary father figure to Sarah, always told her that getting an education was the most important thing a person could do. He told her that education was the one thing no one can torture out of you; education is the ticket to a good life. But for these girls—Sarah knows eight and presumes there are more—marriage marks the end of their schooling. Child brides are walled off to the world, and the promise of their future is robbed from them. The project of Sullivan, of Sarah and her colleagues, stands against that. Sarah has seen it happen before and it sickens her: these girls get married and disappear from Sullivan forever.

Sarah is still haunted by one student who slipped away.

Habiba, a Rohingya refugee from Myanmar, was fifteen years old when Sarah first started to notice a change in her. When Habiba started the school year, she had been one of Sarah's bubbliest and most dedicated students. She spent most of her lunch periods with Sarah and would volunteer to stay late after school to organize papers, pass out flyers, or help with any task that Sarah set her to. That winter, when Sarah collected old winter jackets from her own family and friends to give to Sullivan's refugee students, she gave Habiba first pick— she took a North Face insulated coat. But by January, Habiba's demeanor began to sour. She visited Sarah less often and went days absent from school. When Sarah did pass her in the hall, Sarah would make sure to say hi and ask Habiba how she was doing. Habiba always responded with the same curt answer:

"Good, Miss. Thank you."

By February, Habiba rarely showed up. Sarah decided to confront the girl. When she asked Habiba to explain why her grades and attendance were slipping, the freshman threw her arms around Sarah and held on desperately. Without letting go, she told Sarah that her parents were forcing her to get married. Habiba's attendance and grades suddenly paled in significance for Sarah. She spent her entire car ride home in tears, and the next day at school, Sarah asked if she could visit Habiba's parents at home.

When Sarah arrived at Habiba's apartment the following Saturday, Habiba's mother and siblings sat around their kitchen table, but Habiba was gone. They graciously offered Sarah curried chicken, rice, and spiced potatoes. Habiba's mother was kind and gentle. When Sarah asked her directly about whether Habiba was being forced into marriage, the mother denied the allegation. A social worker from the Department of Child and Family Services who later visited Habiba's mother got the same answer: there was no marriage, the mother said, Habiba was mistaken. After Sarah's home visit, Habiba showed up at school only a few more times before the end of the school year. Sarah heard from the girl's friends that Habiba's wedding had been set for June. Just a few days before the end of the year, a few girls brought a picture from Habiba's henna night. She looked miserable.

The summer passed before Sarah heard any more news of Habiba. The next time Sarah saw Habiba, the girl was pregnant. She gave Sarah the news, adding also that her sixteenth birthday was just around the corner.

In the eyes of the law, it's not obvious that an arranged marriage constitutes kidnapping, or trafficking. Within CPS, awareness of the practice of parents marrying off their daughters, some of whom are as young as fourteen, is new. Teachers don't even know how to spot it or, more importantly, how to anticipate it. One problem is that there is no paper trail. There are no marriage licenses or certificates. These are religious marriages; they are not recorded at the Cook County Clerk's

Office. The girls don't write anyone to say they've changed their names or addresses. At Sullivan, the closest document to an official record is a student's slip in attendance. No matter how many levels of ELL these girls pass, or Dua Lipa songs they learn, no matter how much the Sullivan staff tries to prepare them for the American mainstream, their parents can derail them at any moment.

The practice of matching up child brides happens to grow out of the deepest hopes and fears of parents who are themselves victims and witnesses to the world's worst horrors. It's a practice they may have brought with them from home, carrying with it one of the few remaining links to the lives that were ripped away from them, often in the most brutal ways that humans suffer. They hadn't intended to flee their countries and come to America. They didn't choose Chicago, or Sullivan. It can, and does, terrify them, and, in their traditions, they find solace and an autonomy that is unavailable to them in most areas of their new lives. But, for Sarah, it's the job of Sullivan to give her refugee students what she believes is the best shot at the best life in their new home. And child brides get the opposite of that.

The Illinois Department of Education mandates that all public-school teachers report abuse. Reporting it to the Department of Child and Family Services would begin a chain of events that can create a more stable situation for students, but also has the potential to cause families irreversible harm. If she were to report Shahina's story, a caseworker would visit Shahina's apartment within twenty-four hours of Sarah's call. The caseworker would question her mother, stepfather, and neighbors—anyone who interacts with the girl on a regular basis. They would assess her living situation, which Sarah knows, like those of most refugees new to the country, counts as extreme poverty. She would also need to call World Relief, the refugee resettlement agency that has supported Shahina's family since they landed in Chicago in 2016. The agency would play the role of interpreter, translating the DCFS agent's questions into Burmese. They'd report the family's answers back to the social worker. If the agency concludes that a child is unsafe in their home, it may immediately place the child with relatives or in the foster care system.

So much gets lost in translation. And for refugee families who have often been harassed, perhaps even tortured, by men in uniforms and coercive officials on their way to the United States, bringing in DCFS, or any kind of formal investigation, under the cloud of abuse can be cruel and damaging. Further, Sarah has seen families deceive investigators to prevent further interference into their home life. A call to DCFS is unlikely to offer Shahina relief.

In Shahina's case, the girl's trauma unfolded more than a year ago, and while Shahina's story is horrific, she is now back home with her mother and in no immediate danger. Should that change, and Sarah knows it well could, Sarah, as a mandated reporter, will be required to report the girl's situation to DCFS.

Sometimes Sarah imagines calling her brother, a contractor in Chicago. Together, they would draw up a blueprint for a renovation that would transform her single-family home into three separate apartments—one on each floor of the house—all equipped with their own bathrooms, kitchens, and sets of bedrooms. Next, she would buy the fastest internet she could afford and put range extenders on every floor. She would hit every thrift store in town—Goodwill, Salvation Army, Village Discount—and buy up beds, blankets, and pillows. Sleeping bags, too. She'd then tell girls about to be married off to visit her office at school one by one, where she would lay out the details of her plan. She'd instruct them to pack a bag and tell their parents they'd been picked for a special Sullivan exchange program for promising students. Sarah figures she could cram as many as twenty girls into her house. She would keep them in school and help them find jobs. She'd encourage them to date and teach them about safe sex. She would tell every single one of them that they deserve a future they want. She'd drill into them that they don't get forced into marriage before they even know how to drive. Or are even old enough to drive.

The fantasy isn't perfect. Sarah doesn't like the savior-teacher trope and she doesn't consider herself one. Even when she has brought such cases to DCFS, her impact goes only so far. Parents lie. They say there is no marriage or that the arrangement is the daughter's choice. That leaves not only Sarah, but all those involved in the girls' lives—refugee resettlement agencies, friends, counselors, employers—with little ability to help.

But Sarah still tries. The next time Fatima Peters brings up Shahina's poor attendance and grades, Sarah's answer is simple: "I'm not ready to give up yet."

ZAKIAH

•

Shahina never imagined she'd leave Yangon, the capital city of Myanmar where she was born and raised until age fourteen. The Yangon Shahina knew was a landscape of jarring juxtapositions. The streets boasted a mix of old and new. Painted stucco neo-classical buildings—remnants from the country's long history as a British colony—sat next to golden pagodas while lush streets were lined with jazz-age mansions. The perimeter of the city was marked by the Yangon Circular Railway, a crowded train where monks in maroon and nuns in pink and saffron rode among city residents who carried bundles of tamarind and mango to city markets.

Shahina lived at Yangon's center in an apartment where both Zakiah and her grandmother were raised, too. Despite a decades-long military junta that had transformed much of the lush, resource-rich state into a closed-off impoverished society, Shahina's world was somewhat isolated from hardship. Her grandmother ran a successful real estate business and both Shahina and Zakiah were raised wealthy, by Myanmar standards; there were drivers and maids and plenty of space.

Zakiah hadn't planned to raise her daughter in her childhood home, but when her marriage to Shahina's father fell apart—he walked out of the house after a fight and never returned—Zakiah had no other option. She resented living with her mother, who she felt expected Zakiah to take care of her.

Zakiah was considered ethnic Indian, a class of Muslims brought into Myanmar by British colonists who had become relatively well integrated into Burmese society. Because of her situation, she was considered a divorcée, a designation that held her back. While she spent several years working as a salesperson for a makeup company, Zakiah, together with her mother, determined that she had a better chance at a new future in Malaysia, where jobs were plentiful, the pay better, and where she could escape the stigma of her ruined marriage.

Shahina was six when Zakiah moved to Ipoh and left her daughter in the care of her grandmother. In Ipoh, a popular tourist destination in Malaysia with a world-renowned culinary scene and hawker markets, Zakiah worked in a restaurant where she rolled fish balls for soup. After several months, Zakiah took a job at an iron-welding factory. There she met her future husband, Samad. He was a Rohingya refugee working in the country temporarily and hoping for resettlement. As part of a group of deeply stigmatized rural Burmese Muslims who had been ineligible for full citizenship under the military junta, Samad, like some 150,000 registered Rohingya refugees in Malaysia, had fled there to find work. Zakiah knew her family would not be happy with the match. Marrying Samad meant marrying below her class, so Zakiah waited to tell her mother about the marriage. To Zakiah's surprise, her mother was accepting of her daughter's choice even though it meant Zakiah would likely never return to Myanmar where discrimination against Rohingya grew increasingly dangerous.

In the years since Zakiah had left Yangon, ethnic Burmese Muslims, and particularly the Rohingya people, had become increasing vilified under Myanmar's Buddhist government. In 2012, Rhakine, the Myanmar province that was home to much of the country's Rohingya and Kaman Muslim populations, erupted in violence. Villages were razed across the province and Rohingya families were buried in mass graves. The violence against Burmese Muslims only grew worse in the following years. Reports of mass slaughters across the province started to make headlines, including one outbreak that left ten Rohingya headless, their corpses bobbing in a water tank. The attacks marked a surge of government-sanctioned discrimination and violence against the Rohingya in Myanmar, acts that would eventually lead to an exodus of over one million Rohingya to neighboring countries such as Bangladesh and Malaysia.

Like so many Rohingya refugee families in Malaysia, Zakiah's and Samad's lives remained in limbo. Rohingya refugees—Zakiah now identified as one—still faced great prejudice in their adopted home. The country provided next to no aid for refugees and denied them the right to work. The Malaysian government charged for health care and most Rohingya, including Samad, were left to find jobs in the country's shadow economy. Rohingya children were also barred from attending government schools and private ones proved expensive. Samad continued to work as a welder, but he instructed Zakiah to leave her job. He told her that a wife's job is to stay home and take care of the home. Zakiah acquiesced, but with only one low-paying job between them, the two often had to forgo meals in order to save enough to pay rent.

Hoping to escape life in Malaysia, Samad applied for official refugee status with the United Nations High Commissioner for Refugees in 2013. Resettling in a new country, Zakiah was told, could promise protection and access to work and schools. But the process, which included several rounds of screenings, vetting, and interviews, could take at least two years. Zakiah sent for Shahina. She wouldn't leave Malaysia without her. When Shahina arrived in Malaysia, however, her mother's new life shocked her. Zakiah and Samad lived in a tiny apartment on what Shahina considered scraps. After six at night, the one-room apartment stayed dim until morning. The family scrimped on electricity to have enough money for phones, their lifelines to home and the UNHCR, which was handling their appeal. Shahina was also expected to wear a hijab, which she had never done while living in Yangon. The demand irked her so she spent most days texting with friends back in Yangon and talking to her grandmother on the phone. Shahina begged her mother to return her to Yangon where she had attended private school and had her own driver. She wanted to reclaim the life she'd left behind. Zakiah answered her daughter's frustration by reminding her of the promise of the United States.

In 2016, Samad achieved official refugee status. He was told he and his family would be resettled in Chicago. Zakiah knew little of the United States, but the promise of education, jobs, and a place where she and her husband could live freely inspired optimism. Perhaps Zakiah could reclaim some of the life she'd lost. Shahina, too. But for Shahina, moving to the United States simply meant that, for the second time in her life, she found herself uprooted, but this time to half a world away.

10

MAY

Shahina and Aishah

On a warm spring afternoon, the sidewalks on Devon Avenue throng with a jumble of Sunday shoppers. Parked cars line the streets, many of them boasting license plates from nearby states. Families travel for hours to shop here. Devon is a Chicago thoroughfare busy with Indians, Pakistanis, and Somalis, with Orthodox Jews, Sikhs, and the city's vast mix of Christians, such as Egyptian Copts, Guatemalan Pentecostals, and apostolic Nigerians, all of whom have churches nearby. Shopping bags fill with ingredients for curry, biryani, vegan Egyptian stews, and Sabbath challahs. Twenty-three-dollar fifty-pound bags of rice are universally popular. On the surface, busy Devon is Chicago at its best. Here Islamic bookstores stand a few feet from sellers of Hindu statuary and a local Rohingya center endorses a Jewish congresswoman. The sun is out for the first time in days, and the street is a cacophony—car horns, bhangra music blasting from store speakers, the squeals of children biting fried, sweet Burmese dough balls rolled in sesame seeds and stuffed with rice and coconut sugar. Though it's mid-afternoon on Sunday, this is Shahina's first time out of the house since Friday.

Shahina breathes in the fresh air. The crisp wind offers a welcome change from her family's cramped apartment. At home, Shahina has no personal space. The living room, where she spends most of her time, centers around a small rug, where her two-year-old brother, who was born with a birth defect that has left his arms without hands and with legs that taper off after a few inches, spends his days squirming on the floor. The boy was born while Shahina's family was on the run. At nearly two, he remains mute—half of his tongue is lodged too fully in his throat. The apartment kitchen is a sink and a microwave that rests on a shoddy shelf. Often the only food items in the house are individually wrapped Burmese sponge cakes, instant ramen, and half-empty bottles of orange juice.

Despite the small, cluttered space, Shahina and her mother rarely interact—the two go weeks without talking—and when they do, Zakiah brings up marriage, curses her daughter's obstinacy, and pushes her to land a husband.

Shahina takes advantage of today's outing by donning her favorite dress, a long red polyester button-down with ruffles at the shoulders and a black belt clasped at the waist. She's paired it with a black wool-blend hijab, a braided choker that she's stretched across her forehead, and a small, furry, baby-pink purse. She's painted her lips hot pink and intensified her eyes with pitch-black contact lenses that ring her pupils with tiny white dots that catch the light.

The sophomore has plans to meet Aishah in an hour. First she wants to visit her favorite shop, Pakistan Fashion. The boutique, no bigger than a walk-in closet, brims with scarves, belly dancing garb, and bangles in seemingly every color. Once inside, Shahina runs her fingers across the chiffons, polyesters, and silks, feeling their textures. She pulls out several jewel-tone dresses stitched with plastic crystals and rhinestones down the bust. She stops at a tunic meant for a burka ensemble. Like the girls at Sullivan from Afghanistan, Congo, and Guatemala, Burmese girls have their own shopping strips where they blend Yangon styles with those of Chicago teens. Zakiah has urged Shahina to wear more conservative tunics, but so far, she has refused. She doesn't even like wearing a hijab; she prefers to wear her hair down. Shahina pledges to herself that she'll jettison the scarf when she lives on her own—which is to say, not with a husband she's been rushed to find or one forced on her.

Leaving the store, Shahina makes her way toward a string of jewelers. She passes by several of the shops, deeming their styles too traditional or too garish. Or at least, the wrong kind of garish. But after a minute, she stops. She leans into a window to see a display of necklaces, her nose nearly touching the glass. At the center stands a collar with sheets of yellow gold fanning out from a central pendant like birds' wings. The piece looks like the one she wore at her engagement party last year. She shudders.

Chicago's Burmese community is small, and Shahina knows people judge her choices. Whenever she talks about the past, she tends to look over her shoulder, checking if anyone is eavesdropping.

The topic of gossip remains front-of-mind when Shahina arrives at Ghareeb Nawaz, a Pakistani restaurant on the eastern end of Devon Avenue. Shahina and Aishah gather here often after school. The two became close after they met at a friend's birthday party at a Kentucky Fried Chicken. The food, they agreed, though not halal, tasted delicious. Soon, they discovered they spoke the same two languages—Burmese and Complaining-About-Their-Mothers. The spacious Pakistani restaurant is a favorite among Muslims, especially taxi drivers, who fill the tables in the early morning hours after their overnight shifts. But today, families—grandmothers in *shalwar kameez* bouncing grandchildren in their laps while reining others into their chairs—discuss the week's gossip in a babble of languages: Arabic, Rohingya, Urdu, Farsi, and more. Aromatic curries waft from the vast, populous kitchen where white-smocked and square-hatted men churn out dozens of dishes—frontier chicken, *tikka paratha*, *chili gosht*—beloved in part because full plates cost less than $5. Coming to Ghareeb Nawaz is a kind of ritual for Shahina and her friend. They can spend hours here, sitting over plates of food, reminiscing about the watermelon juice, beef satay, and papaya salad sold on the streets of Yangon.

Today, the two friends pool $13 between them. Aishah works at the neighborhood Jewel-Osco grocery store and always sets aside a few dollars from her paycheck for these outings. Moving down the long steel cafeteria counter, they settle on a chicken biryani; it comes with a mountain of rice, and a plate piled with *paratha*, an Indian fried wheat bread. The two dishes should be enough to last them through dinner, they figure. Neither of the girls plans to go home before 8 p.m. After ordering, the duo settles into a table toward the empty back of the restaurant, removed from eavesdroppers.

"You remember when I called to tell you I was engaged?" Shahina asks Aishah, launching right in.

"I was so shocked," responds Aishah, "and sad."

"You didn't even believe me."

"Yeah, but also, I kind of did, since my mom did the same thing to me."

During her freshman year at Sullivan, Aishah, now nineteen, fought off a suitor her parents picked for her. The man was in his early thirties and lived downstairs from Aishah and her family. He would sometimes say hello to Aishah, then sixteen, in the hallway. He asked her about her day and for news from school. It started off innocuously, but later gifts began appearing at her door; a new iPhone, then a gold ring, and eventually a new set of Bose headphones. He waited for her in his car outside Sullivan. He'd follow Aishah home, calling her name and telling her to get in his car. When he told Aishah's mother that he wanted to marry her, Aishah was adamant that she would not marry him. But Aishah's mother encouraged her daughter to accept the proposal. She said that marrying a wealthy man would help secure a good future.

"They always just want you to marry the rich guy," says Shahina.

"Yeah, my mom was like, 'You won't have to work. You won't have to worry about nothing. Just do whatever you want. You will live like a queen.' But really, that guy was like a wolf." This wasn't the first time Aishah encountered such an aggressive man. Aishah's mother wed Aishah's father in an arranged marriage, despite the fact that he already had two wives, one in Thailand and another in Laos. Aishah has also seen her father hit her mother. "You have to protect yourself from guys like that."

"This would never happen in Yangon. Most people marry when they're like twenty-three," adds Shahina. "That's a normal age. This is happening because we're in America. Our parents, they're scared that we're in America. They're scared that we're changing."

Shahina shrugs and digs into the plate of biryani. Just then, her phone dings. It's a Facebook message from a boy—not the kind of boy her parents have in mind for marriage.

The boy is tall, with a strong jaw and thick, black hair. He travels among the Asian Boyz gang, a group made up mostly of fellow Rohingya refugees. The boys have been increasingly drawn to American gang culture. Sarah is aware of the problem; she's had the words "gang intervention" written on her office whiteboard since January. One reason she hasn't yet confronted the crew is that she figures their interest is mostly cosmetic. But she still finds the phenomenon bewildering. How is it that boys who watched Buddhist soldiers burn their villages are enamored with, and bewitched by, Chicago gangs? Other refugee kids, like the Congolese who left town, run to steer far away from gangs. The tall boy Shahina likes, and his pals, however, may find that gangs offer power, money, status, and community—qualities that could attract any young person who feels a sense of powerlessness.

Shahina finds herself drawn to these boys. In her eyes, they are dangerous and unpredictable—two qualities the seventeen-year-old craves. She and the Rohingya boy have been texting on Facebook all afternoon. Despite being drawn in by bad behavior, Shahina sticks to less treacherous topics: music, scary movies, and her favorite foods. The two trade messages about their families. Dozens of texts are just strings of emojis that have grown into inside jokes. They laugh about certain friends' chastity and others' indiscretions and send each other plenty of selfies. They swap less-than-scenic photos taken in the cafeteria, the classroom, by a windowsill, and from the library floor. In other words, they flirt like other teenagers. But for Shahina, the stakes of such behavior are high.

Shahina looks up from her phone. She waves at a young woman, no older than eighteen, who has just walked through the door dressed in a smattering of pastel colors topped by a baby pink hijab. Trailing behind her are two small children and a forty-something man.

"Like that," says Shahina raising her eyebrows as though to convey shock. "She was forced to marry that guy when she was fourteen. Now she has two babies."

"She looks so sad," adds Aishah. "She could be his daughter."

"I'm not going to get married," continues Shahina. "My mom doesn't believe me, but I'm going to show her that I can live my life without a husband."

"Our parents all think we need men for our future," says Aishah, "but what about woman power? We can live our lives on our own."

"My grandma always told me I have to learn to stand up on my own," says Shahina. "She said I shouldn't ever be dependent on a man."

"We're going to work and make our own money," says Aishah. "We're going to travel."

"To Burma, Paris, Singapore, and the pyramids in Greece."

"You mean Egypt," laughs Aishah. "We are going to make our own future."

Ramadan

Dear colleagues, as most of you are aware, the holiday of Ramadan starts this week . . . I'm writing to explain how this tradition affects the school day and offer my services in helping with difficult conversations that may arise. These students fast from sun-up to sundown, which means they wake up around 4 a.m. and do not eat dinner until about 9 p.m. Many students will be tired or crabby. The library is open during all lunch periods as an alternative to the cafeteria. For example, gym class . . . Given that these students cannot drink water, it might be thoughtful to send them to the library as an alternative to a two-mile run assignment. If you find an obstinate student, or you feel a student is using Ramadan as an excuse for inappropriate behavior, please do not hesitate to contact me. And I will speak to them.—*Sarah M. Quintenz*

"I can't go on this field trip because I'm going to be too hungry," Abdul Karim, a Syrian senior, complains, referring to a school visit to a food pantry. He's trailed by a pack of boys, most of whom appear puffy eyed and sleep deprived. They're certainly tired, but they're also playing it up. One by one they slam their bodies into the chairs around the center table in the ELL "womb." Abdul Karim, wearing a gray hoodie over a Sullivan T-shirt, sits in the corner beneath the window. Another tilts his chair toward the door. He wears a backward baseball cap, white shorts, and an empty bag of Bold Party flavor Chex Mix over his left hand like a mitten. "Tomorrow is the first day of Ramadan, I'm going to be so hungry."

"That's bullshit," Danny Rizk replies, strategically placing himself in front of a large standing fan. "A field trip like this is the actual point of Ramadan."

In Chicago, Ramadan comes with the arrival of late-spring humidity. The city's cool spring can pass quickly into summer. The streets are again lush and green. Sparrows and pigeons can be heard through the Sullivan windows, which remain open throughout the school day to let air into the stuffy hallways. In the library, students have traded their heavy winter coats for lighter fair. Girls who sported thick hijabs are now covered in pastel cottons. While March temperatures imbued the Sullivan hallways with a spring giddiness, the mugginess of May has dampened it.

"But I'm going to be so tired, man," Abdul Karim persists. "Why they making us do this during Ramadan?"

Sarah enters the room. She's heard enough to jump in without hesitation. "Nobody helped you in your home country? Nobody helped you in America? No one ever helped you?"

Abdul Karim laughs. "No . . ." he says sheepishly.

"Boy, I'm going to . . ." Sarah cuts herself off. "We can't go feed starving people tomorrow because we're going to be starving because it's the first day of Ramadan? Come on."

"A student told me that we practice Ramadan because God wants you to know how to live as people without much food and water," adds Danny.

"Yeah, that's true," Abdul Karim nods.

"So, shouldn't helping people in that state during Ramadan make even more sense?"

"I understand, but tonight I have work at 7 p.m.," retorts Abdul Karim, who works at Cairo Nights, a neighborhood hookah bar. "I'm going to finish at 5 a.m. tomorrow. I'm going to sleep two hours and then come to school. I can't go out in the sun after fasting and working."

"So then say that," says Sarah. "Say, 'I'm not going on the field trip . . . '"

"Okay, yes," Abdul Karim responds, cutting Sarah off.

"Stop interrupting," she demands. "What you're teaching people is that you can't feed the homeless because of Ramadan. That sounds bad, man."

"Yes, okay, I understand."

"How am I supposed to quit smoking with shit like this?" Sarah says as she rises from her chair. She pats her jacket pocket for cigarettes. The box is there. "Don't follow me," she snipes over her shoulder as she heads toward the school parking lot.

On Wednesday, the day after the field trip to feed Chicago's homeless, Abdul Karim is back in the ELL office, trailed by his friends. They break into laughter as soon as they enter the room. Two of the boys explained they've broken their fast because they gawked at a classmate's breasts.

"The first look is halal," one explains to Sarah, referring to an action considered permissible in Islamic practice, "but the second look? Haram."

The idea makes Sarah burst into laughter. "I'm going to put that on a T-shirt. It doesn't matter what language you speak or culture. Boys are boys."

Sarah has spent two years trying to help the Syrian seniors, one of a recent wave of Muslim students to Sullivan, negotiate boundaries between typical public school experiences in Chicago and the religious and cultural expectations they're accustomed to. For many refugee students, attending Sullivan is their first exposure to secular education. In the United States, sticking to a secular curriculum is mandated by law. Yet, for the traumatized groups who land at Sullivan's doors, religion can provide a powerful sense of comfort and security. And conflict with their religious practice can be deeply unsettling. At Sullivan, the times for two of the five daily Muslim prayers are hard to miss. A chorus from students' mobile phones sounds throughout the school announcing the call to *salat*. That's why, after fielding numerous requests from Muslim students asking to leave class for prayer, Sarah created two spaces for just that. The girls were offered a second-floor classroom and the boys a small room just off the school's main auditorium. They could pray, but only if given a hall pass. Sarah often reminds students not to take advantage of the compromise.

But for Abdul Karim, who comes from a conservative Muslim family, no change inside Sullivan can recreate what he's lost since forced out of Homs in 2012. On Thursday, the boy returns to the ELL office. He looks tired, the circles under his eyes a soft shade of maroon. There's no levity in his voice today.

"I don't really feel Ramadan anymore," he says to no one in particular. "I just don't really feel it like I did before."

In Homs, the thirty days of Ramadan were Abdul Karim's favorite part of the year. It was when he felt closest to God. He began and ended his day at the mosque, rarely looking at the clock. The *adhan*, sung out over microphones across the neighborhood, marked the passing hours. There were four prayers between sunrise and sunset, between Abdul Karim's first and last meal of each day.

During Ramadan, all of Homs seemed to slow and relax. The days were filled with naps and prayer, and the aromas of his mother's cooking. She ensured that the family had a feast for the breaking of each day's fast. Just the typical accouterment—baba ganoush, hummus, grilled flatbreads, fattoush salad—took a couple of hours to prepare. The main dishes, including *mahshi*, or cored eggplants, zucchini, or squash stuffed with spiced rice and minced meats; kibbeh, made from bulgur, onions, and finely ground beef; freekeh and chickpea salad; and lentil soup, consumed the rest of his mother's day.

The iftar, or breaking of the fast, came on the heels of the fourth prayer. When it did, the entire city seemed to shut down. Businesses closed. Restaurants shuttered their blinds. Everyone stopped their days to first eat something sweet—to revive from low blood sugar—and then came the evening feast. Most nights, at least eight people gathered around Abdul Karim's family table. Together, they began their feast with dates, a fruit eaten by the prophet Muhammad, and tamarind juice, yogurt, or *erk sous*, a sweet and bitter tea made from licorice root. As a boy, Abdul Karim fantasized about eating every dish spread across the table. His eyes were inevitably bigger than his stomach. He rarely finished his plate of food.

After iftar, the neighborhood poured onto the sidewalks and streets. *Fanous*, Ramadan lanterns symbolizing hope, cast a yellow glow onto the dark streets. Under their light, groups—mostly men and boys—gathered to smoke hookah, play chess and cards, or challenge one another in games of pickup soccer. Abdul Karim was never without his cousins or siblings. Everyone seemed to move in unison. He felt safe. Moreover, he never felt alone.

When Abdul Karim recalls those long nights spent on the streets of Homs, they feel like another life. His first Ramadan in Chicago hit him hard. In the city, there was no call to prayer. He tried praying at the neighborhood mosque, but he found it filled with strangers, so he resigned himself to praying at home. At school, he was often tired and frustrated by the eight-hour-long school days. In Syria, he had only six classes, each of them forty-five minutes long. American school always felt long, but while he fasted school days felt more than tiring, and sometimes debilitatingly lonely. From school, he'd go directly to his job working at the hookah bar. He'd break his fast at an empty table, shoveling spoonfuls of leftovers that his mother had prepared the night before. In Homs, the entire fasting month felt like an extended meditation. But now, in Chicago, the grief of his exile runs deep.

Friday arrives. On Fridays during Ramadan, observers are expected to pray together with their community. Abdul Karim has heard that a new math teacher, himself a practicing Muslim, will lead prayer in his classroom. It's unclear how the arrangements began. Public schools are prohibited by law from organizing religious worship for students, but students themselves have a right to organize gatherings and to pray on their own. At Sullivan, with the refugee children, no one presses the issue.

Rather than go home to pray, Abdul Karim heads to the makeshift prayer room. To clear the floor for kneeling worship, desks, still piled with calculators and backpacks, have been pushed to the front of the room, the chairs stacked around them. Below the desks, the students' shoes, most of them sneakers, make their own haphazard piles. On the wall, a poster reads "I am me—I am okay."

Abdul Karim removes his shoes and jacket. He takes a small yellow rug from the corner, one from a colorful stack donated to the school. He lays the rug between two of his classmates. Their rugs face toward the qibla, the direction all Muslims face during prayer in order to face the Holy Mosque of Mecca. Abdul Karim uses "Qibla Compass," a phone application, to determine the correct orientation. To Abdul Karim's left, stands a Rohingya sophomore and to his right, a Somali junior. They stand in a line just a few feet behind the math teacher who leads the group.

The prayer begins. The boys raise their hands and say, in unison, "Allahu Akbar" or "God is great." They place their left hands over their right and bow forward as the teacher leads. He then turns around to face the boys and offers his preaching or "khutbah."

"We're now a few days into Ramadan," he begins. "If you're not feeling anything yet, it's not really a concern. It takes time. Eventually, we should feel a different type of spiritual sense within ourselves. And if you don't, that is okay."

Just then, the three descending notes of the school announcements blast from the classroom speakers.

Coach Williams, if you're in the building, please meet Livingston in the main entrance.

The teacher continues calmly, unfazed by the interruption. "Like I said, it takes time. Get some rest this weekend. Just keep doing your best. Keep showing up. And also, do your homework."

The math teacher then turns back around to face the same direction as the group. He begins the recitations again.

When the prayer finishes, Abdul Karim returns his mat to the corner. Before he exits the room, he nods to a few of his classmates and encourages them to visit him at work. He grabs his backpack. It's heavier than usual, weighed down by the provisions from his mother. He's not sure what's in the sealed Tupperware, but it doesn't matter. It's a taste of home, and Homs. When Abdul Karim arrives at Cairo Nights, he will have just under an hour remaining before he can eat. Inside the dim bar, where the walls are decorated crimson red, and the now empty tables and chairs sit waiting for hookah smokers, only the app on his phone will signal when day turns to night and he can eat. When he learns the sun has finally dipped below the horizon, Abdul Karim will recite the fourth prayer, open his sealed plastic box, and eat every last bite of the dinner his mother prepared.

Shahina and Aishah

By mid-May, Shahina has stopped showing up at Sullivan altogether. She's determined to have her own apartment and to find a job that will pay her enough to begin saving for it. Living under her mother's roof, Shahina believes, is no longer tenable. Earlier in the month, Shahina was hired by a small shop stuffed with cheaply made traditional Indian and Pakistani dresses and jewelry. She worked during the week for $4 an hour cleaning the storage room and restocking displays. The hours proved grueling and customers asked her one too many times what size bra she wore. Shahina quit after just one week, but she never returned to school.

Since quitting the job, Shahina spends almost every day bouncing from one neighborhood fast-food chain to another—anywhere employees won't scold her for using their free WiFi. She's almost always accompanied by Aishah, who now has missed nearly as many school days as Shahina.

On a foggy May morning, Shahina arrives at a strip mall Dunkin Donuts just after 10 a.m. wearing jeans and a black top. She's taken the time to fill in her eyebrows and brush her lips with an orangey-red lip stain. She knows that the chain's Coolattas, sweet blended coffees, will erode her perfectly lined lips, but Shahina has arrived prepared. Her lipstick is stashed in her purse.

If Shahina were at Sullivan, she'd be well into third period. Several of the tables are occupied by regulars, one of whom has collected the free papers from outside the store and spread them into a patchwork of paper across his table. Another emerges from the bathroom looking more wasted than when he entered it. Shahina stands at the counter, craning her neck up toward the illuminated menu on the wall behind the counter. She has no interest in observing Ramadan. She plans to order an Oreo-flavored Coolatta to share with Aishah when she arrives.

Aishah lives a mile from Shahina. Her family's apartment is a larger version of a typical Chicago railroad-style unit where several small rooms jut off a long, narrow hallway. There are three bedrooms—one of which her parents often rent for additional income—and a proper kitchen. The apartment has a dining room big enough to hold a dining table that can easily sit eight, but which is almost always stacked with toilet paper, groceries, and cleaning supplies. Though Aishah has more corners to disappear to, there's nowhere at home she feels safe. Her father, who works night shifts cleaning airplanes at O'Hare International Airport with Shahina's stepfather, is rarely home, but when he is, the house erupts in violence. In the early hours of the morning, Aishah hears her father blame her mother for Aishah's misbehavior followed by the sounds of slammed chairs and loud slaps.

"This is your fault," she'd hear her father scream. "You don't discipline your daughter."

The fights have become more frequent in the last few months. The stress has irritated Aishah's acid reflux, a pain so sharp she barely sleeps. When she sits awake at night, she texts Shahina. She's the only one Aishah texts. The girls often text each other until sunrise.

The situation for Aishah has gotten so bad that she started reserving some of her salary and giving it to her mother in secret. When her mother asked her why she was giving her money, Aishah told her, "So you can leave."

Aishah knows her mother will likely never leave her husband. Aishah, however, is dead set on getting out.

When Aishah walks through the door, she carries a backpack that holds her Jewel-Osco uniform, a makeup bag, and a cell phone charger. She doesn't intend to return home until well after dark.

Shahina is already sitting at a high-top against the window. The table is covered in daily tabloids, almost all of which speculate about the "Royal Wedding," or the upcoming nuptials between American actress Meghan Markle and Prince Harry. Shahina pushes the papers aside and slides the Coolatta over to her friend who takes a sip. The routine is a familiar one.

The two spend the next few hours side by side, but on their phones. The only times they look up are to dissect a mutual friend's post or snap photos of each other. One frequent topic the girls discuss is their hope for the future, almost as though articulating their dreams out loud keeps them alive.

"I heard most people in America move out when they turn eighteen," says Shahina, turning to Aishah. "They get their own money and have their own house. That's what I want."

"It would be really cool if we could live together," Aishah adds. "If we do that, we won't feel like we're being controlled. Last night my mom told me again that I need to marry. I felt like my head was really burning. I was so angry, I just said, 'Don't force me to marry. I'm giving you money. I'm giving you five hundred dollars a month to help you. Don't tell me what to do.'"

Shahina and Aishah like to imagine the apartment they'll rent together. In their own apartment, they would stay up late watching horror films. They might even have parties. And even if their apartment has nothing in it, they agree, it will be better than living with their parents.

By mid-morning the girls are ready to switch locations. They consider where they could go next. Shahina suggests McDonald's, where they can each order a one-dollar soft-serve ice cream. As they walk south down Clark Street, the sidewalks are crowded with people. The sun has come out from behind the clouds and the sky is a bright blue. Standing on the sidewalk curb, the girls hear a loud boom. Two cars have crashed in the middle of the street—one T-boning the other. Both drivers emerge from their cars, one of whom falls to his knees in despair. His car is likely totaled. Shahina and Aishah link arms as they observe the scene.

"You know, my parents always tell me that I'm going to die a horrible death," says Aishah. "Like worse than I can imagine. They say it every day. Especially during Ramadan."

"Mine, too," adds Shahina. "I came into this world alone and I will leave it alone."

"Except me," says Aishah, pulling Shahina's arm closer to her. Shahina laughs. A crowd has begun to form around the two smashed cars. The girls decide to continue walking. As they do, they move at a slow pace, watching traffic speed by and soaking in the sun.

11

JUNE

Alejandro

Alejandro stands over a small altar for his slain friend Jose. He's assembled a jar candle virgin and a photo of Jose, a young man with a thin mustache, on the cusp of adulthood. He dips his head down, closes his eyes, and prays. He prays here every night. This small corner of Alejandro's room is his church. He prays for his family. He prays for the sick. He prays that he'll remain safe in America. News from the border has been grim for months. In early May, more than two thousand children had been separated from their parents after crossing into the United States. The separations were introduced as part of the Trump administration's new immigration policy that asserted a "zero-tolerance" for illegal border crossings. That also included prosecuting parents traveling with their children as well as people who attempted to request asylum.

Alejandro climbs into bed. His nights have been restless, and he knows he won't sleep tonight. When he closes his eyes, disordered images of Guatemala flood his mind: his mother's house, rivers he swam in, friends, many now dead. In preparation for his day in court, Alejandro has spent the last several weeks trying to memorize the details of his journey to the United States and of what propelled him. The query frustrates Alejandro. If he could return to Guatemala safely, he would already be there. He'd wake up to his mother's pupusas and walk streets full of the familiar smells. He could see his friends again and watch his sisters grow into women. How can he communicate how much he'd like to go home if there were a good chance he'd escape the gangs? One wrong date or detail in court tomorrow, Alejandro fears, could cost him his life.

From his bed, Alejandro can see his black suit hanging in the closet. His father, Sergio, had it pressed and cleaned, and it now hangs under a protective plastic dry cleaning bag next to the black Air Jordan sweatshirt that Alejandro wore the night he fled Guatemala. He received the hoodie the Christmas before he left, and wore it for the first time when he went to join his father. He wanted to arrive in the United States in his best clothes. He never wears it anymore; it doesn't fit.

Sergio told Alejandro he cannot dirty the suit; he has to wear it for both his court date and his Sullivan graduation on Wednesday. Alejandro and Sergio had spent the day together. They first hit a barbershop just south of their apartment, where the barber, a Guatemalan man who had cut Sergio's hair for years, asked Alejandro what style he preferred. Alejandro explained he had to appear in court. The barber nodded knowingly. His technique was old school. His long black comb moved through Alejandro's thick hair as the fast, muted scissors reshaped Alejandro's shaggy top into an unthreatening cut for court. No fades or razor patterns and just enough pomade to keep his hair in place. The loss of his ponytail hit harder. He hadn't trimmed it in years, hoping that his mother would be the one who finally cut it when they met again. But Alejandro's lawyers insisted that he clip it, and he relented. Once Alejandro was brushed off and treated with talcum powder, Sergio paid and they both thanked the barber. Sergio took his son for a *caldo de res*, a beef soup made with potatoes, corn, jalapeños, and topped with lime and cilantro. He knew the soup would comfort Alejandro. It wasn't Luana's recipe, but it wasn't bad, either. Sitting at the table, the two talked about sports and graduation—any topic that wasn't Alejandro's court hearing or his hair. But the next day weighed heavily on them, and by the end of the meal, they ate in silence.

Struggling to sleep, Alejandro has his mother on his mind. He wishes Luana were with him in Chicago. He wishes he could talk to her. Nearly four weeks have passed since they last connected by phone. A recent volcanic eruption in Guatemala City left her with feeble internet access, and texts were the best they could do. The last message she sent him read: *I will pray for you. Everything will be OK.*

When Alejandro's alarm sounds at 7 a.m., he's still awake. He didn't sleep at all. After showering, he fits into his suit. His freshly starched shirt feels crisp against his skin. He promised to walk his girlfriend to school this morning, but they'll have to walk slowly so he doesn't sweat through his jacket. When the two arrive at Sullivan, Alejandro stops by the library. He looks in vain for Sarah. Alejandro had considered asking Sarah to accompany him to court but decided against the idea. He'd rather go alone. A student asks him why he's wearing a suit. A funeral? Job interview? He shrugs, avoiding the question. Sergio calls. He's parked outside.

Sergio won't join Alejandro in court. He's heard rumors that U.S. Immigration and Customs Enforcement agents have made a habit of stationing themselves outside courthouses to arrest undocumented individuals accompanying their family members. While schools, hospitals, and places of worship have effectively been off-limits for federal immigration officers, courthouses have not. And because of reports about the marked increase of ICE activity in courts over the past two years, many, like Sergio, no longer feel safe going anywhere near them. It is simply too risky. But he'll drive Alejandro to his lawyers' offices. When they pull up outside the downtown building, Sergio turns to Alejandro. "I'm going to pray for you. Go do your best."

Alejandro and his two lawyers spend the next two hours reviewing his answers one last time. The two women are thorough and matter of fact, but also give him hope. Before they leave for the courthouse, one of the lawyers collects Alejandro's file. In it, there's a letter of support from Sarah. She writes:

> [Alejandro] is a selfless and mature man; it is hard to believe he is only eighteen years old. . . . [Alejandro] is a person who cares very deeply for the feelings of others and is cognizant of how he can leave the world a better place than he found it; [Alejandro] truly embodies *cura personalis*. I believe this intense empathy for others stems from the fact that [Alejandro] immigrated to this country when he was thirteen years old. He knows what it's like to feel lonely and scared. . . . And, like most refugees, [Alejandro] would tell you that he would return to Guatemala—return to his mom, siblings, and friends—if he felt like it was safe to do so. But he also knows what it feels like to dream and have ambitions—and this is where [Alejandro] focuses his energy and talents. He does not lament his struggle or blame others for his defeat. [Alejandro] will clearly, and unequivocally, tell you he has been blessed with an opportunity and he plans to waste no time in creating a meaningful life for himself and his family.

Alejandro is already thinking past the hearing. If he is denied asylum and the judge orders his deportation, Alejandro would have to act quickly. Someone told him he could marry his girlfriend, who is an American citizen. The idea irks him. He doesn't want to marry for the wrong reasons or put that pressure on his girlfriend. He could stay and continue to work without any legal status. Continuing to work as an undocumented immigrant is obviously not ideal, but it's better than a death sentence.

In the early afternoon Alejandro and his two lawyers cab it to the courthouse. It stands at the corner of two busy streets in the heart of the Loop, Chicago's main business district. The elevated train rumbles and screeches above the sidewalks as the cars drive over the tall, rickety tracks. Every sound seems amplified to him now. Are these the sounds of his past or will they fill his future? A steady stream of people pour in and out from Union Station, Chicago's imposing old central train station. Many carry wheeling luggage. Perhaps they've just arrived in Chicago. There's a Starbucks across the street and a deep-dish pizza joint a little farther south. It feels like the city is passing him by, a blur from the taxi window.

Inside the federal building, Alejandro and his two lawyers take the elevator to the fifth floor. When they arrive at the hall leading to the courtroom, they put their belongings down on a security conveyer belt and walk through a metal detector. Just like at school. He does the same every morning when he enters the Sullivan building. America is safer for him than Guatemala, but the regular scanning reminds him it's not all that safe. There are seven courtrooms, one for each judge, spread along a labyrinthian corridor. The floor has no windows or plants. It's not unpleasant, but it gives little face to the bureaucracy. Each courtroom has a small waiting area with sets of chairs, some bolted to the floor, others freestanding. Alejandro sits and waits for his lawyers' instructions. Just beyond the doors, the courtroom is empty. No one occupies the wooden benches in the gallery or the two long tables just beyond the gate that divides spectators from the lawyers, the subject of the hearings, and the judge's high bench. The witness stand is vacant, too. When the court is next occupied, Alejandro's future will be at stake.

Even before the room fills, however, Alejandro's heart begins to pound. *Please God, make this fast,* Alejandro says to himself, holding his hands in a prayer formation against his chest. He prays. *Dios mío, no deje que esta gente me mande de vuelta a Guatemala que no quiero regresar.* Or, "My God, don't let them send me back to Guatemala, because I do not wish to return." His fear swells. He tries to breathe deeply to slow his heart.

A few minutes pass. The room remains oddly empty. Usually, the waiting area is filled with individuals waiting for their cases to be heard. The quiet adds to Alejandro's anxiety. Something's amiss. So far, the only person he's seen on the fifth floor is a security guard. Time seems to slow.

Alejandro's lawyers approach him. They look angry. They tell him that his court date has been pushed back—again. Across the country, nearly eight hundred thousand immigration cases are waiting to be resolved, and most of them need a judge to determine whether they can stay in the country. There are only fifty-eight immigration courts across the country and every single one of them has a massive backlog. Alejandro's lawyers explain to him that they should have a new date soon. The two women keep talking, but Alejandro can't keep track of the details. His head buzzes. What he does understand is that he will continue to wait. His fate won't be settled today. Later that summer, his lawyers would send him his new court date: August 2021.

On Wednesday, when Alejandro's alarm again rings, he is already awake. He dons his black suit and pulls his polyester navy-blue graduation robe out of his closet. It's a good day. He will graduate. And he's alive, and he's in America.

Alejandro arrives at Loyola University, the big campus on Lake Michigan, not far from Sullivan, and the site of graduation. The sidewalk is lined with vendors carrying balloons, flowers, and stuffed bears in small red buckets. Alejandro files behind some of the other students heading into the auditorium, disappearing into the sea of blue, yellow, and white gowns.

"Alejandro," Sarah calls out from somewhere in the crowd. She comes barreling over and throws her arms around him. "I'm so proud of you. I wish your real mom was here, but I love you like my own family." He smiles in the embrace. Yes, he does wish his mother were there, but Sarah, he feels, does love him. He will take a lot of pictures and tell Luana all about graduation later.

The group of graduates gets antsy as they wait for their cue to enter the auditorium. Lauren, who is headed to University of Maine on a scholarship, stands nearby in a white robe and cap decorated with numerous tassels—a distinction reserved for honors students. She beams from both elation and sweat. It's hot.

Later in the summer, Lauren will settle into her new dorm room and discover a love for lobster rolls. She'll study anthropology and fight for environmental justice. She'll write poetry and immerse herself in early Hollywood films. She'll find it challenging to build community where less than 2 percent of students are Black. The word "outsider" will take on new, acute meanings. But for now, standing in the packed lobby surrounded by her Sullivan classmates cloaked in their graduation wear, Lauren feels invincible.

Nearby, Alejandro drips with sweat. When the ceremony finally begins, he lines up, standing parallel to a classmate. As he walks into the hall, Alejandro holds his head up. A smile of satisfaction stretches across his face. When he takes his seat, the sun shines through the big stained-glass windows and Alejandro's row alights with a glow of colors. The ceremony begins with students welcoming the room in a medley of languages. Next, Joe Moore, the city alderman for Sullivan's ward, steps to the microphone.

"This is the face of America," says Moore. "We have every single nationality in this room. . . . This is not the end. This is the beginning."

Chad speaks. So does Matt Fasana. The valedictorian talks. Mayoral candidate Lori Lightfoot—who will go on to win the election—takes the microphone.

"When I look out on this incredible crowd, I see what is best about our great city. You reflect our hope for today, tomorrow, and a brilliant future. Your diversity, your distinction, and your passion for the city, for the school, and for learning is infectious. It really gives me hope about what we can accomplish together."

Sarah leans against the metal railing at the back of the auditorium. She recently gave her own spin on Lori Lightfoot's speech when she tracked Aishah down. Aishah had been one of Sarah's best students when Sarah still taught. She had nominated the junior for the school's honors medical program. Not only was Aishah accepted, but before she started skipping class, she was one of the top students in the program. Sarah wasn't willing to lose Aishah, so she asked the girl's teachers to each write a letter encouraging her to return to school. Sarah delivered the letters to Aishah herself. When Sarah knocked on Aishah's door, the girl was home without her parents, caring for her younger siblings. Aishah's head was uncovered and her siblings zoomed from one end of the apartment to the other, screaming with delight at their unexpected visitor.

Sitting in the living room, Sarah dove right in.

"How come you're not coming to school?" she asked.

"I have some problems," Aishah answered coyly.

"Are you pregnant?"

"No."

"Is someone hurting you?"

"No."

"Are you hurting yourself?"

"No."

Sarah decided to take another approach.

"Aishah, you are smart," she said. "I really believe in you. You need to go to college. I know you think I'm just saying these things because I'm your school mom, but other people believe it, too." Sarah handed Aishah the letters. "I hope you decide to come back. We miss you."

Back at Loyola, Chad reads off the names of the Sullivan graduates. Students file across the stage to receive their diplomas. Alejandro is among the first. He walks with a noticeable boost in his step. His mother often told him that only 10 percent of teenagers in Guatemala graduate from high school. He takes his diploma, descends the steps, and walks back to his seat.

Standing on the lawn after the ceremony, Alejandro takes dozens of pictures. One with every teacher who helped him make it across that stage. In each of them, he stands, relaxed, his cheeks flushed from the heat, looking directly into the camera. He keeps his smile mild, never widening his lips more than a millimeter, but his eyes are alert, even delighted.

Chad Adams

For Chad, the school year never ends abruptly. Rather, the sounds of shoes and slamming locker doors seem to dim to silence. First the seniors leave, then the rest of the students. For a few days at the end of June, only teachers remain in the building. Then they leave, too. In the end, Chad shares the halls with only a few other staff.

As Chad takes a seat in his second-floor office, the summer sun lights up the room. Opening the window, he listens to the birdsong. He sees a sign posted in the yard of a handsome, single-family house across the street. It's one in a multihued row of single-family homes painted in mint green, taupe, robin blue, and it's for sale. He's considering making an offer for it.

Lately, Chad has been upbeat and the idea of buying a new home grows from his optimism. He's graduated his second senior class at Sullivan and the school is taking a turn for the better. In April, Chad received the school budget for next year. He told the district that Sullivan would likely house more than 700 students next fall, the largest number since Chad took over as principal. He pointed to the school's growing attendance and rising ranks among public high schools. His efforts paid off: The new budget came in at a record $4 million. It covered 720 students, or nearly 60 more than the 2017–18 budget.

Turning Sullivan around from a school with a 44 percent graduation rate to one where 90 percent of freshmen remain on track to graduate in four years has been one of the hardest lifts of Chad's career. But now, he can boast a jump in college-bound students and a drop in suspensions. He can celebrate the school's better ranking, and the fact that, for the first time in over a decade, it's no longer on probation within the district or under threat of possible closure. He can also now use some of the new budget to hire additional staff, bolster school programs, and update a few of the school's tired facilities.

As a former English teacher and high school and college athlete, Chad has a coach's chest of metaphors that describe his plans for Sullivan: Sullivan has made the playoffs, but to really make the school great, Chad must bring the place to the World Series. He wants Sullivan to be the best-performing neighborhood high school in Chicago. And he has a specific data set in mind: 90, 90, 90. A 90 percent graduation rate matched by a 90 percent college enrollment rate at a high school where 90 percent of students qualify for free or reduced lunch.

The first students Chad met in his first days at Sullivan were a group of refugees participating in a summer program. They were students who had landed in a school, in a city, and in a time, that put them at the center of the American project. They were the newest Americans. And Chad knew, if he succeeded in his vision for Sullivan, they would become tough, multilingual, multicultural thinkers who could help America's future. Now, five years into his tenure, Chad feels he is finally fulfilling that promise.

Before the teachers left for their summer break, Chad shared his excitement in a speech to his staff.

> At Sullivan, we know who we are. We know where we're going. I want you all to walk with that Sullivan swag. You should walk with that S on your chest and be proud to be part of this school. Wear that S with pride. We've gone from the lowest-performing school on the North Side of Chicago to a school with rising attendance, enrollment, and graduation rates. Look at this. Look at what we did. Be proud.

But Chad knows better than to dwell on any one success. That's why he's kept written records throughout his fifteen years working inside CPS. Looking over his entries, Chad is reminded how radically different his life looks from when he left Harper High School five years ago. He still keeps Harper's shield-bearing insignia on his keychain. It reminds him of his hardest days. They may still haunt him, but they also fuel him.

Soon, Chad will write his fifth Sullivan entry. That's as long as he's been at any one institution, and he feels as though the school has become a part of him. His inner clock is the school's clock, even when he's not at the school. It's also reshaped his psyche because unexpectedly, while he's connected to everyone at Sullivan, as principal, he feels in some ways more isolated and lonelier than he could have imagined. Other principals must feel that, too, but none have ever confided that in him, let alone prepared him for it. The pressure to keep an entire school afloat weighs heavily on Chad. The future of his students does, too. Good news buoys him, but he knows reversals will come, too. And he feels the troublesome trends taking shape in the nation will threaten the education and safety he can offer his students. The excitement of a success can quickly turn to a desperate desire to hold on to it.

Chad's cell phone buzzes. It's the guitar repair center. They tell him that his "baby" is ready. He plays in several bands. Hot as Hell, a Jesus and Mary Chain-cum-Queens of Stone Age band, remains his longest-standing group, and another punk group in which Chad goes by the stage alias Principal Pleasure, has a few gigs booked over the summer. The fun of Chad's alter ego is a declaration to himself to never linger on the negative. In the band he can briefly push aside the internal rhythms set by Sullivan. Pumping out a punk barrage on his guitar can also help hurdle him forward. It is a phase that he calls *Let's fucking go*. Alice Cooper said it another way, but the meaning is the same: *School's out for summer!*

12

AUGUST

Belenge

Stacks of mismatched plates and glasses fill several super-market boxes on the sidewalk outside the building entrance. A small mountain of black trash bags stuffed with donated clothes and shoes stands next to them. Chicago is a convection oven in August, and thermal drafts carry the stink of trash and other aromas drifting down to the sidewalk. From Belenge's family's third-floor apartment, drift the smells of bad plumbing and the sweat of moving day. The building door is propped open so Belenge, Asani, and a squad of friends can carry their remaining belongings down to the street. Belenge's family has decided suddenly to leave Chicago.

Belenge's father, Tobias lost his job earlier in the spring. Since then, he's collected unemployment. Though Belenge rarely stays at his family's apartment, when he does, he finds the trash bin filled with bottles. Then there's the smatter-ing of beer cans around the air mattress that Tobias sleeps on. Tobias's drinking wasn't new, but his speed at draining the bottles was. If he wasn't drinking, he was likely at Mama Sakina's house sleeping it off. One afternoon in early August,

Tobias lay on Mama Sakina's couch, asleep, while one of her daughters played on the floor next to him. Without waking, Tobias rolled off the couch and onto the floor with a loud thud. The girl yelled for Mama Sakina, who discovered that Tobias was barely breathing. A 911 call summoned an ambulance, which took Tobias to St. Francis Hospital. Belenge was told his father's organs were failing. Tobias spent nearly a week in the hospital. When he was released, Tobias decided to move his family to Lansing, Michigan, home to a small Bembe community including some of Tobias's cousins. He reasoned that if he fell ill again, his cousins would help take care of his children. When Tobias broke the news to Belenge, the boy felt his life in Chicago, and especially at Sullivan High School, was being stolen from him. He felt his father was making them all run again, when there was no real enemy but alcohol. But in the end Belenge realized that they were destined to move on.

On the sidewalk outside the apartment, a small crowd forms. Word has spread that Belenge and his family are leaving Chicago. Theirs is the latest of a series of departures by Congolese families. First Esengo and his family relocated to Iowa. Belenge rarely speaks to Esengo anymore, but he's heard that his friend suffers from symptoms of post-traumatic stress disorder when he recalls the evening of October 13. That night scared many in the Congolese community and pushed several families to move to Kentucky and Wisconsin. Even Mama Sakina says she plans to move her family to the small Wisconsin city of

Appleton once she finds an apartment there. Belenge wonders who will remain in Chicago come December.

Though a shooter has not been identified, and Esengo's case remains among the 95 percent of unsolved shootings in Chicago, the fears that rattled Belenge at the beginning of the school year have faded. For months, he got rides to and from school, but by the end of the year Belenge was back to walking. The sounds of spring construction projects and honking horns served as his soundtrack. He'd started to like school, too. His English teacher has been taking the class on field trips to learn not only vocabulary and grammar, but also about life in America. In May, Belenge and his classmates walked to the neighborhood grocery store, Devon Market. It may have been a small outing, but it was a big adventure for him. Once they arrived at the store, Belenge stood just inside the entrance, his mouth slightly agape. As he surveyed the crowded aisles, his eyes widened. Never had he seen multiple varieties of bananas or red, green, and yellow apples. There were piles and piles of greens, each one with a different leaf, shade, and shape from the other.

"What are these?" he asked once inside, holding up a nut still in its shell. Someone pointed to a sign above the bin. "Almond," he read out loud. He had never heard of such of a nut. Walking over to the butcher counter, he saw a mix of Italian hot sausage, chicken, pork rubbed with Mexican chiles, and heaping bins of ground beef. On top of the counter sat a display of plastic bags filled with chicharróns. He recognized chicken feet from Mama Sakina's cooking. There were so many new and familiar wonders inside the store. The neighborhood—now his neighborhood—held copious mysteries and delights.

Moving to Lansing means that Belenge may not visit Devon Market again. He doesn't know if he'll ever return to Chicago, either. Gloria Walsh, the American volunteer, has the trunk to her car wide open. She and her nephew have offered to drive Tobias, Belenge, and his siblings to Lansing, in two cars. It's nearly time to go. Despite some creative stuffing, barely half of their belongings—mostly clothing—fit into Gloria's nephew's car. Tobias was told to leave all the furniture from the apartment upstairs, because it was infested with bed bugs. The clothes probably are, too, but he's grown attached to them.

The trip is about to take the family through American Midwestern towns, places whose stories are told in songs and on cereal boxes: Gary, Kalamazoo, Battle Creek. But Belenge will be a stranger to them all. He will sleep through almost the entire four-hour drive to Lansing. If he wakes, he'll be greeted by cornstalks at their full summer height and billboards pointing to exits for gas, country buffets, fast food, and twenty-four-hour Christian hotlines. *What's a Culver? Is there really a ButterBurger?* When they reach Lansing, the buildings will look small compared to those in Chicago. And commercial strips with too many empty storefronts will look desolate compared to the big city. When their car pulls up outside a white single-family house, a group of familiar faces will meet them outside. Belenge will recognize his cousins and an elderly family friend, whom he calls Grandmother. He'll notice a huge tree with big branches that bounce over the driveway. Out back, he'll see bicycles piled in a corner and a bouncy ball resting in the dirt. The house they'll come to belongs to a man Tobias refers to as his younger brother, but he isn't.

Inside, two women will stand in the kitchen stirring large vats of beans and beef stew. And, of course, there will be *fufu* on the stove. Familiar smells will fill the house. The group will gather in the sparse living room, each person taking from the home's own collection of mismatched plates, likely also donated through a refugee agency, school, or church. The two cooks will carry the pots and dish a ladle full of stew and another of beans onto each plate. As the group eats, Belenge will fall exhausted into a chair, thinking about whether this new place will or can ever feel like home. Whether he will live there, and if his father will die there, in peace.

That's all to come. Before they leave Chicago, Belenge says his goodbyes, one fist pound or handshake at a time. When he climbs into the car, he rolls down the window. Sounds of the city flood in. The elevator train rumbles and screeches. Kids on bikes call out to one another as they pedal furiously up and down the block. The neighborhood has more than its share of cars on life support, and the frequent sound of their stubborn ignitions is sending the family off, too. Looking around the busy street, so many elements that once intimidated Belenge really did come to feel like home. As the car pulls away, each grows smaller in the rearview mirror.

EPILOGUE: SEPTEMBER

Sarah Quintenz

The new school year is off to a troubled start. When Sarah arrives at Sullivan, she learns that before sunrise, the first floor flooded leaving the halls covered in two inches of water. It's 7:55 a.m., just before school would usually open, and some of the flooding has yet to be mopped up. That means the doors won't open at eight. A crowd of waiting students and some parents are pushed together outside Sullivan's front doors. Others form in a line down the block. There's the giddy trading of summer stories and gossip. Some students worked, others seemed to have devoted their off months to mastering the game Fortnite. Everyone is eager to get inside but as the opening time passes, a murmur of confusion takes over the story swapping.

Mariah, now a junior, arrives one minute past 8 a.m. She takes her place at the back of the crowd, nearly half a block from the school doors. She's wearing light blue jeans and a matching jean jacket; her hair is straightened and her backpack hangs off her right shoulder. No hijab this time. She also wears her new camel-color, faux suede high-top sneakers.

She bought them with money from her job working at a neighborhood diner. Mariah had enrolled in summer school but didn't stick with it. Her second eldest sister, who has spent the last several years in college and working part-time for an airline company, is now engaged to one of the girls' cousins in Kuwait. She's set to get married abroad in December.

When the doors open, students spill into the school lobby. All must put their backpacks through the metal detector. A typical first-day bottleneck forms, and some students know the drill while others look bewildered. Mariah waits patiently. She's not particularly eager to get inside. As she ascends the front steps, she reaches for the door and holds it open for a few students.

This year Mariah will manage the boys' basketball team; try, then quit, the poetry club; run track; and, taking on a big responsibility, help organize the school's Martin Luther King Day assembly. That will give her an interest in event planning. She'll become a leader on Sullivan's Student Voice Committee where she'll advocate for her classmates by pushing for better cafeteria food and doubling her efforts to eliminate school uniforms. She'll also discover the digital media room and meet Nassim in the process. At first, the two will joke around only in English, but eventually, with time, Mariah will begin to tease her friend in Arabic, too.

As Mariah lets go of the door, she pulls her backpack off her shoulder. "Can't turn back now," she says, following the crowd inside.

Inside, Sarah, Josh, and Danny Rizk stand just outside the library. They wave to returning students and shepherd new ones into the library and tell them to wait. As feared, there are fewer new refugee students. Judging just from the crowd in the library, now full of seasoned refugee students, most of whom completed one or two years in a Chicago middle school before coming to Sullivan, they seem more at ease, less frozen, less lost than the first-day crowd in previous years. They will need help and guidance, of course, but they don't look like they'll need much rescuing. Noticeably absent are the usual bunch of students who have newly arrived in the country. Everyone knew this would come and have consequences for the ELL program's funding. What's a little less expected is the deeper disappointment. Those brand-new, wide-eyed refugee students will be missed. Sarah turns her focus to the students who have returned. Last spring, Chicago Public Schools renewed her program for two more years, after which she fears the school within a school that she spent years building up will probably collapse.

As students push through the hallway, Sarah spots a Syrian junior in the crowd. The boy walks with a kind of "wild and crazy guy" confidence and Sarah erupts into laughter. Of the 260 students she hopes will return to Sullivan's ELL program, Sarah never expected to see this boy, a particularly obstinate student with a wide variety of disciplinary problems, again. But he is surviving all the setbacks and challenges, including Sarah, who is constantly needling him for his cocksureness.

"No fucking way," says Sarah. Josh and Danny look over. They laugh now, too.

"Wow," adds Danny. "Did not see this coming."

The boy approaches the trio. He asks for his new schedule.

"Today is the first day of your new life," says Sarah, grinning. "It's a new year."

Sarah waits anxiously to see if Aishah will walk through the doors. She knows she won't see Shahina today. The Burmese girl chose to transfer to Senn High School where she will repeat her sophomore year. Shahina wants to start over, but not at Sullivan. Sarah still holds out hope for Aishah.

At last, at a few minutes past 9 a.m., Aishah walks through the doors. Sarah, who sits at the card table where returning students fetch their new schedules, jumps up from her seat.

"Oh my god!" she cries. "You came back!"

Aishah smiles, her hands pressed against her stomach. Her acid reflux has not subsided. Sarah's visit had moved Aishah. And in her lowest moment, when she felt resigned to give up on school, the gesture helped her see that there were still people who believed in her. She didn't want to disappoint them, or herself. "I came here to study and I need to go to college."

"Right on," Sarah says, throwing her arms around the girl. "But you're late. Get going. Have a good year."

After Sarah sends Aishah off to class, she turns toward the library. Inside, a host of students and families wait to register. Scanning the room, she considers where to begin. The room is full of students who Sarah will come to know. They are students who will flirt, dream, work, and try on different personalities, fashions, and spiritual practices. They will perfect TikTok dances and memorize BTS K-pop hits. They will face racism and cope with challenges of urban poverty and oppression. They will become Sarah's extended family, and she theirs. But first, enrollment. Sarah only lingers in the doorway for a moment. Then, without hesitation, she marches toward a shy-looking girl hovering by the back windows. She'll start there.

AUTHOR'S NOTE

In January 2017, just a week after Donald J. Trump was inaugurated into the presidency, thousands of protesters gathered inside Terminal 5, Foreign Arrivals and Departures, at O'Hare International Airport in Chicago. They held handcrafted banners with slogans like "No One Is Illegal." Groups of Muslim immigrants waved signs that read "We Are Not Terrorists." Together, everyone chanted "No Trump, no KKK, no fascist USA." Cowbells rang. Drums were beaten. Just a few hundred feet away, 150 volunteer lawyers planted themselves at the airport's McDonald's tables and advertised free legal representation to anyone who had family members who had been detained at customs and put in custody. Under the harsh, fluorescent lights, a palpable sense of urgency, anger, and hope hung in the air.

That same month, hundreds of protests erupted across the country in response to Donald Trump's executive action blocking travel from seven majority-Muslim countries and suspending all refugee resettlement for 120 days. Within his first eight days in office, the president had made good on his threat to set a new, anti-immigrant, "America-first" agenda for the nation. Standing among the crowd at O'Hare, I wondered: *What does this political shift mean for those refugees and immigrants who made it off the plane? What kind of America will they inhabit? What kind of America will they help build? And how will America take shape around them?*

Those questions prompted me to search for a story about immigrant and refugee life in my hometown of Chicago. A few weeks later, a friend, and former Chicago Public Schools principal, tipped me off to Roger C. Sullivan High School. In the 2016–17 school year, Sullivan welcomed more refugees than any other high school in Illinois. I paid a visit to Sullivan. Standing at the end of the high school's long hallway lined with flags from around the globe and welcome signs written in more than a dozen languages—Arabic, Swahili, Spanish—I was in awe. I knew the story of Sullivan was one that was both urgent and timeless.

I spent the next three and a half years reporting what would become this book. It started with a *Chicago* magazine article in June 2017 titled "Welcome to Refugee High." For that piece, I spent several months inside Sullivan. While there, I found myself enwrapped in the stories of students who had suffered years of horror that they often kept inside. Their resilience was remarkable. But they were also, in many ways, typical teenagers. This was a realization that both delighted me and challenged my preconception of the refugee experience. Their lives were swirls of Rihanna, acne, and gossip mixed with Turkish

pop, midday prayer, hijabs, and bottle-blonde hair. I wanted
to know these students and understand their stories.

In September 2017, I began to report the book in earnest. My
first step was identifying the four students who I would follow over the next year. I spent an entire school year following
Mariah, Belenge, Alejandro, and Shahina. I shadowed each of
them both in and outside of school. I spoke with them in the
library and ate at their neighborhood restaurants. I watched
YouTube on their couches and shopped at their favorite stores.
I sat in their bedrooms and attended family gatherings. They
became part of my life and I theirs.

I also spent time with each of the student's parents. I listened as they shared stories from the lives they left behind.
Mariah, Belenge, Alejandro, and Shahina may not always
agree with their parents' choices, but I felt it important to
understand their perspectives. They have, after all, made great
sacrifices to provide a better life for their children.

In total, I conducted hundreds of hours of reporting. Everyone featured in this book agreed to participate. The scenes I
did not personally witness were reconstructed from in-depth
interviews and secondary documentation including videos,
emails, police reports, and notes taken by first-hand observers.

Because this book deals with teenagers and their families who stand among the world's most vulnerable, I decided
to use pseudonyms for them in the book. I am so grateful to
those who shared their stories, and I felt it was important to

protect their trust. I recognize it is a privilege to have this platform and I'm grateful for it.

Since finishing my reporting, I have kept in touch with both students and Sullivan staff. While the shifting political tides loomed over the city back in 2017–18, no one could have predicted how the world would change in the coming years. Over the course of four years, the Trump administration introduced a suite of blatantly anti-immigrant, anti-refugee policies including an expansive ban on work visas and a 49 percent reduction in legal immigration. The administration also established an annual ceiling for refugees that was 84 percent lower than the final year of the Obama administration. As of July 2020, only 7,848 refugees had arrived in the United States in fiscal year 2020. But there remains reason to hope. In January 2021, President Joe Biden signed a suite of executive orders on immigration including ones that lift the travel ban, end the national emergency declaration that diverts money to border wall construction, and change arrest priorities for Immigration and Customs Enforcement. He announced his intention to reestablish America's commitment to refugees and set the annual global refugee admissions cap to 125,000.

In Chicago, the once-crowded Sullivan hallways now sit nearly empty as everyone reports to school from home due to COVID-19. Sullivan's English language learner funding continues to shrink as does its number of refugee students. But for the students and teachers of *Refugee High*, life marches forward. Both Mariah and Belenge graduated in June 2020. Mariah enrolled at Wilbur Wright College, a community college in Chicago where Aishah is also a student. Belenge now works at a recycling center in Appleton, Wisconsin, where he moved with his siblings and father after graduating. Shahina remains in search of love, and Alejandro works in maintenance. He still hopes to become a mechanic and buy his mother a house. Sarah Quintenz continues to chair Sullivan's ELL department, which has shrunk to six members. She also has a new partner with whom she had a daughter in 2020. Chad Adams, who now goes by Chad Thomas, launched a $25 million project to address the numerous issues plaguing the nearly hundred-year-old Sullivan building. Ever the optimist, Chad still holds his vision for Sullivan close. And now, thanks to a renewed contract, he has until at least 2025 to execute it.

No matter what shape America takes in the coming years, Sullivan will continue to carry forward this country's long tradition of welcoming newcomers. The story of Sullivan High School reflects a better America, one that offers sanctuary and second chances to those who need them most.

ACKNOWLEDGMENTS

This book would not have been possible without the cooperation of Chad Adams, Matt Fasana, and Sarah Quintenz. They were brave to let me into their story and did so with the hope that it might make a difference for their school and their students. I am also grateful to the entire Sullivan High School ELL department, who did not shy from asking me hard questions about my intentions and process. They care deeply about their students, and I appreciate their trust.

I owe so much to Mariah, Belenge, Alejandro, Shahina, and their families, all of whom shared their stories and tables with me. I was, and remain, deeply moved by the generosity of those who have experienced the world at its worst. There were many others who welcomed me into their lives and homes, including Aishah, Abdul Karim, Ihina, and Lauren. They, too, were a constant source of inspiration.

So many have championed this book from the start, but a few people deserve particular mention. To Terry Noland, for believing in the original idea and giving the book its name. To Clare Fentress, for weathering the proposal process with me. To Nate Sivak, Trudi Langendorf, and Gloria Walsh for answering copious calls and texts and for their friendship. To Alex Kotlowitz for his generosity and wisdom. To Annette D'Onofrio and Natalia Piland for their wonderful, thorough edits and advice. To Bill Gerstein for alerting me to Sullivan High School, and to Alisa Wellek for her insight. To Niclette Kibibi, Yara Meerkhan, and Sarah Hunaidi for their kind and exacting notes.

To Ben Woodward, my thoughtful, erudite editor, who was a true collaborator and who has become a friend. To my agent, Andrew Wylie, who encouraged me to write this book and who fought for it, too. And to everyone at The New Press, I'm so thankful you let me tell this story.

Many thanks, too, to my friends and family who have nurtured me and my career; I have always felt buoyed and bolstered by you. Thank you to Jessica Stern, Brenda Fowler, Gioia Diliberto, Jennifer Tanaka, Jonathan Eig, and Dan Buettner for their guidance. And to the ladies in my life who showed up in Chicago, Montreal, and Milwaukee, and in ways far too numerous to name.

I am also indebted to the International Women's Media Foundation and the Awesomeness Grant for their support. And to my research assistant, Bashirah Mack, for her brilliant work on this project. To Lily Chavez and Michael Blackmon for fact-checking the book.

Finally, thank you to my dad, Ted, for inspiring me to write and guiding me along the way. And for his unvarnished critiques. To my mom, Sara, for everything, including her genes. To my brother, Adam, for his support, sensitivity, and for Sequoia. To my cousin Emily for answering every call and for always making me laugh. To my aunt Nancy for her advice and enthusiasm. To my grandmother Elaine for being the most insatiable reader I know. And to Jonah Gaster, my husband and partner, for always cheering me on and up. For listening and loving, and for all those buttermilk chickens. I couldn't have done it without you.

ABOUT THE AUTHOR

Elly Fishman worked as a senior editor and writer at *Chicago* magazine. Her features have won numerous awards including a City Regional Magazine Award for "Welcome to Refugee High," her first report on the students and faculty at Chicago's Roger C. Sullivan High School, from which this book grew. A Chicago native and graduate of the University of Chicago, Fishman currently lives in Milwaukee with her husband and their dog and teaches in the Journalism Department at the University of Wisconsin–Milwaukee.

PUBLISHING IN THE PUBLIC INTEREST

Thank you for reading this book published by The New Press. The New Press is a nonprofit, public interest publisher. New Press books and authors play a crucial role in sparking conversations about the key political and social issues of our day.

We hope you enjoyed this book and that you will stay in touch with The New Press. Here are a few ways to stay up to date with our books, events, and the issues we cover:

- Sign up at www.thenewpress.com/subscribe to receive updates on New Press authors and issues and to be notified about local events
- Like us on Facebook: www.facebook.com/newpress books
- Follow us on Twitter: www.twitter.com/thenewpress

Please consider buying New Press books for yourself; for friends and family; or to donate to schools, libraries, community centers, prison libraries, and other organizations involved with the issues our authors write about.

The New Press is a 501(c)(3) nonprofit organization. You can also support our work with a tax-deductible gift by visiting www.thenewpress.com/donate.

THE STUDS AND IDA TERKEL AWARD

On the occasion of his ninetieth birthday, Studs Terkel and his son, Dan, announced the creation of the Studs and Ida Terkel Author Fund. The Fund is devoted to supporting the work of promising authors in a range of fields who share Studs's fascination with the many dimensions of everyday life in America and who, like Studs, are committed to exploring aspects of America that are not adequately represented by the mainstream media. The Terkel Fund furnishes authors with the vital support they need to conduct their research and writing, providing a new generation of writers the freedom to experiment and innovate in the spirit of Studs's own work.

Studs and Ida Terkel Award Winners

Catherine Coleman Flowers, *Waste: One Woman's Fight Against America's Dirty Secret*

Lawrence Lanahan, *The Lines Between Us: Two Families and a Quest to Cross Baltimore's Racial Divide*

Janet Dewart Bell, *Lighting the Fires of Freedom: African American Women in the Civil Rights Movement*

David Dayen, *Chain of Title: How Three Ordinary Americans Uncovered Wall Street's Great Foreclosure Fraud*

Aaron Swartz, *The Boy Who Could Change the World:
The Writings of Aaron Swartz* (awarded posthumously)

Beth Zasloff and Joshua Steckel, *Hold Fast to Dreams:
A College Guidance Counselor, His Students, and the Vision
of a Life Beyond Poverty*

Barbara J. Miner, *Lessons from the Heartland: A Turbulent
Half-Century of Public Education in an Iconic American City*

Lynn Powell, *Framing Innocence: A Mother's Photographs, a
Prosecutor's Zeal, and a Small Town's Response*

Lauri Lebo, *The Devil in Dover: An Insider's Story of Dogma
v. Darwin in Small-Town America*